To Jessica and Josh –
Hope when you get to Maine
that you can do some of
these things – enjoy –
Graduation 2018

Love you,
Grandma

50 Things
TO DO IN
MAINE
BEFORE YOU DIE

50 Things

TO DO IN

MAINE

BEFORE YOU DIE

NANCY GRIFFIN

Down East Books

Down East Books
An imprint of Globe Pequot

Distributed by NATIONAL BOOK NETWORK

Photographs: Dan Tobyne, except photos on pp. 5, 9, 14 (background), 25, 27, 28, 36, 37, 48, 49, 50, 51, 52 (right), 53 (right), 54, 63, 69, 79, 88, 96, 99, 121 (bottom, 135 (right), 144, 146, 147 (top), 150-51, and 152 © iStock. com; photos on pp. 127, 133, and 145. © Dreamstime; pp. 105 76279890: © Bratty1206, pp. 105 76118202: © Bratty1206, pp. 69 52265156 © Americanspirit, pp. 133 44555444 © Marpit, pp. 126 1041246 © Kcphotos, pp. 145 30004474 © Jinnee, pp. 66 15835767 © Tashka, Lynda Chilton, pps.13, 14 top, 18, 20, 78,
Book design by Lynda Chilton, Chilton Creative

British Library Cataloguing in Publication Information available

Library of Congress Cataloging-in-Publication Data available

ISBN 978-1-60893-629-8 (hardcover)
ISBN 978-1-60893-630-4 (e-book)

∞™ The paper used in this publication meets the minimum requirements of American National Standard for Information Sciences—Permanence of Paper for Printed Library Materials, ANSI/NISO Z39.48-1992.

Printed in the United States of America

THINGS TO DO

Introduction, *8*

1 ➻ Drink Moxie, *10*

2 ➻ Get a Load of Maine's Favorite Berry, *12*

3 ➻ Illuminate Your Life, *17*

4 ➻ Climb Katahdin, *24*

5 ➻ Watch for Your Ship to Come In, *30*

6 ➻ Shop at L.L. Bean, *34*

7 ➻ See a Whale, *36*

8 ➻ Spot a Moose, *38*

9 ➻ Get Lost in the Desert, *43*

10 ➻ Whitewater Rafting, *44*

11 ➻ Canoe the Allagash, *48*

12 ➻ Eat a Potato, *52*

13 ➻ Learn About the Good Life, *57*

14 ➻ Watch for Puffins, *60*

15 ➻ Witness a Whirlpool, *62*

16 ➻ Pan for Gold, *64*

17 ➻ Build a Boat, *66*

18 → Run the Beach to Beacon, *68*

19 → Go Mushing, *70*

20 → Dig for Treasure, *72*

21 → Catch a Movie at the Drive-In, *74*

22 → Go to the Park, *77*

23 → Sail on a Windjammer, *80*

24 → Make Maple Syrup, *84*

25 → Discover the First Fort Knox, *86*

26 → Catch a Lobster, *88*

27 → Get Tipsy on Allen's Coffee Brandy, *91*

28 → Visit the Shakers, *92*

29 → Enjoy One of the Sweeter Things, *96*

30 → Soar in a Hot-Air Balloon, *98*

31 → Drive Route 1, *101*

32 → Deck the Walls with Art, *104*

33 → Eat Bean Hole Beans, *106*

34 → Make the Most of Monhegan, *109*

35 → Dine at DiMillo's, *112*

36 → Get off the Grid at a Sporting Camp, *114*

37 → Walk in the Gardens, *118*

38 → Become a Champion Tobogganer, *120*

39 → Meet Maine's First People, *122*

40 → Ride in a Seaplane, *127*

41 → Drive a Stanley Steamer, *128*

42 → Eat at Moody's, *130*

43 → Stand in the Clouds, *132*

44 → Hike the Canyon, *136*

45 → Take a Driving Tour of the Solar System, *140*

46 → Listen to Loons, *143*

47 → Hop on a Bike, *145*

48 → Explore the Old Port, *146*

49 → Harvest Ice, *148*

50 → See the Milky Way, *150*

INTRODUCTION

Welcome to Maine, the largest New England state, larger than the other five combined, but only thirty-ninth of all fifty states. Still, it's possible to drive for eight hours or more from one end to the other.

More than half the population lives within 25 miles of the sea, on only one-seventh of the land, meaning if you're not in southern Maine or coastal Route 1 in summer, or in the largest city (Portland),

you may have little human competition for space—not necessarily a bad thing.

If you don't like trees, you're out of luck. Trees cover 90 percent of the land, and Maine is the most heavily forested state.

But if you like water, you're all set. With so many lakes, ponds, and rivers, Maine moves to number twelve in water area, with around 4,523 square miles. And that's not counting the ocean. Measure around the islands and the wrinkled, convoluted coast, and Maine boasts a coastline of 5,200 miles. Plus, there are islands, lots of islands—more than 3,000. A lot can happen on such a coast, and does, from lobstering to fishing to sailing—everything from tiny sailboats that hug the edge of a bay, up to week-long adventures on Maine's fabled windjammer fleet.

LOOKS CAN BE DECEIVING

Maine has so many islands that along certain parts of the midcoast, the Atlantic begins to look distinctly un-ocean-like. The view has prompted more than a few folks from away to enquire, "What's the name of that lake?"

All of this means that Maine has enough land and water to supply travelers with a nice range of adventures, activities, and unique sights to see on foot, or from a car, bicycle, hot-air balloon, motorcycle, or snowmobile. Here are our fifty suggestions of the things that must be done if you want the full Maine experience, covering all four seasons—or, as we say in Maine, "winter and August." Complete 'em all and you're a real Mainer . . . nah, just foolin'; the only way to be a true Mainer is to have been born here. But this is as close as you can get.

1

DRINK MOXIE

Moxie, the soda in the bright orange can with the distinctive (some would say disgusting) flavor, is Maine's official soft drink. Invented around 1876 by Dr. Augustin Thompson of Union, and first marketed as a medicine, "Moxie Nerve Food" was sold as a relief for everything from "softening of the brain" to loss of manhood. The name is said to derive from the Indian word for wintergreen, an ingredient in the moxie, and the soda's unique flavor may derive from another ingredient, gentian root.

Since it promised to provide the drinker with "spunk," the word *moxie* has worked its way into the lexicon, as in "You've got moxie." Moxie is not actually made in Maine, and sells in only a few places outside of New England, but it holds the distinction of being America's oldest continually sold, commercially marketed carbonated drink. It's not always easy to

find in stores, but the brand is owned and bottled by Coca-Cola.

So devoted to Moxie is Maine that there's a three-day festival in Lisbon Falls every July to celebrate all things Moxie. There's a special Moxie collection in the "Moxie Wing" of the Matthews Museum of Maine Heritage at the Union Fairgrounds in Union. Moody's Diner in Waldoboro usually hosts its own Moxie Day just prior to the Lisbon Falls festival. There's even the New England Moxie Congress, a membership group of "Moxie zealots" devoted to the beverage and to collecting Moxie memorabilia.

HELPFUL SITES

- *moxiefestival.com*
- *matthewsmuseum.org*
- *drinkmoxie.com*

The name Moxie appears in at least fifty place names in Maine, including falls and ponds, and some linguists say the word may mean "dark water" in an Abenaki language. Moxie Falls in the town of Moxie Gore (50 miles north of Skowhegan), is Maine's highest waterfall with a single vertical drop of nearly 90 feet, reached by the Moxie Falls Trail.

There is no logical explanation for why a full-sized horse atop an old car—the "horsemobile"—is a Moxie symbol, but the one remaining example of this odd vehicle lives in New Hampshire but turns up every year at the Moxie Festival.

2

GET A LOAD OF MAINE'S FAVORITE BERRY

Maine's official berry, the low-bush, wild (wild because they are not planted but occur naturally) blueberry, grows over 44,000 acres in barrens that range over most of the state. The small wild blueberry is known for its flavor, versatility, vitamins, and powerful antioxidants. At 10 percent of North America's crop, Maine is the largest producer of all blueberries in the world, harvesting some 90 million pounds a year.

If you're here during blueberry season (early August), you can buy fresh, local berries in most supermarkets. There are also farm stands, farmers' markets, or that ubiquitous pickup truck parked on the side of the road with a hand-lettered sign and a card table. After the season, fresh berries will be hard to find, but as a consolation, blueberry fields turn a beautiful scarlet in the fall.

PICK 'EM YOURSELF

A few dozen Maine blueberry farms throughout the state, some organic, allow you to pick your own when berries ripen, usually late July into early September, depending on the weather in any given season. Remember blueberries grow low to the ground, so picking involves a lot of bending over.

OR JUST EAT THEM

Of course, if you would rather just eat them, already made into something delicious, most Maine eateries offer blueberry treats. Blueberry muffins, jams, jellies, pancakes, and pies are ubiquitous. If you're lucky, you might find blueberry melt-in-your-mouth, a light, unfrosted blueberry cake Mainers usually make at home. Local producers are also making high-quality nontraditional blueberry products like maple syrup, wine, chutney, ice cream, and gelato.

CHECK OUT THE WORLD'S LARGEST BLUEBERRY

Columbia Falls, Maine, boasts the world's largest blueberry. It's actually a shop, designed to look like a blueberry, and

nearly everything about it is blue. Built and owned by a blueberry-farming couple, the shop sells blueberry jams, jellies, sauces, vinegars, scones, muffins, cookies, and ice cream. The blueberry dome is the primary attraction of Wild Blueberry Land, a (you guessed it) blueberry theme park. With Maine becoming a "foodie" mecca, local producers are making high-quality non-traditional blueberry products that include blueberry maple syrup, blueberry wine, and blueberry ice cream and gelato.

HELPFUL SITES

- *pickyourown.org/ME.html*
- *visit-maine.com/state/ pick-your-own-farms/ extension.umaine.edu/blueberries/*
- *wildblueberryland.com*

THE BLUEBERRY RAKE

The blueberry rake is a hand-held device that most closely resembles a dustpan with long teeth and a reversed handle. Credit for the rake's invention goes to Abijah Tabbutt of Hancock County, Maine in 1883. The top of the metal rake is shorter than the bottom, so the long teeth move through the blueberry plant, causing a minimum of damage to it. The berries (and a few leaves and twigs) are stripped from the plants into the rake.

Maine's Native Americans dried blueberries to make pemmican, a high-energy food carried by warriors and hunters.

15

3

ILLUMINATE YOUR LIFE
WITH LIGHTHOUSES

Maine's long, wrinkled coastline is necessarily dotted with lighthouses. More than five dozen lighthouses—the second highest number in the country—still flash in the dark and fog to guide sailors safely past Maine's fabled cliffs and rocks as they have for two hundred years.

While the Coast Guard still maintains aids to navigation in Maine, ownership and sometimes operation of the lighthouses now rest in the hands of local agencies or preservation groups. The Maine Lights program, passed by Congress in 1996, led to the transfer of 28 lighthouses from the Coast Guard to local preservation groups or other agencies and served as a model for the National Historic Lighthouse Preservation Act of 2000. Except for eight privately owned towers, all but a handful of Maine's lighthouses now have local support groups, such as Friends of Rockland Harbor Lights.

Maine is also home to a national organization dedicated to lighthouse preservation, the American Lighthouse Foundation, based in Rockland, and to *Lighthouse Digest* magazine, "Saving lighthouse history since 1992."

LIGHTHOUSE STATS

OLDEST: Portland Head Light, commissioned by George Washington in 1791

YOUNGEST: Whitlocks Mill Light, lit in 1910. Also the northernmost in the state and therefore on the United States Atlantic Coast.

EASTERNMOST: West Quoddy Head Light.

TALLEST TOWER: Boon Island Light, but the highest due to land elevation is Sequin Island Light, off the Kennebec River.

SMALLEST: Echo Point Light, nicknamed "Pocahontas." This little 6-footer, located on the edge of Great Diamond Island, is the smallest lighthouse registered with the Coast Guard.

MOST PHOTOGRAPHED: Pemaquid Point Light. It's also on the Maine quarter.

MOVIE STAR: Marshall Point Light in Port Clyde is the spot where Forrest Gump ended his run in the movie of the same name.

Tour lighthouses by boat. From Down East to southern Maine, boat operators offer lighthouse tours, photo ops, and sunset cruises, sometimes incorporating whale-watching or puffin-watching in the trip.

Get a passport. The United States Lighthouse Society issues passports, available in some Maine locations, for lighthouse enthusiasts who want to support the lighthouse preservation effort. Passport Club members can collect stamps at more than 450 locations around the country and receive discounts on future passports. Society members may also receive discounts on select lighthouse cruises.

THINGS TO DO

Sleep in one! On Isle au Haut, you can sleep in the home of the former keeper at Robinson Point Light. The Keeper's House is now a four-bedroom bed-and-breakfast.

Visit the Lighthouse Museum in Rockland. The museum's purpose is is to educate the public about the history of lighthouses and to preserve the stories and artifacts of their lifesaving mission. It houses the largest collection of lighthouse paraphernalia in the country, including sparkling Fresnel lenses. While in Rockland, also take a walk on the nearly mile-long breakwater out to Rockland Harbor Breakwater Light.

HELPFUL SITES

- *visitmaine.net/page/39/*
  lighthouse-directory
- *seathelights.com/me/Maine.html*
- *mainelighthousemuseum.org*
- *lighthousefriends.com*
- *lighthousefoundation.org*
  maine.gov/sos/kids/about/
  lighthouse.htm

4

CLIMB KATAHDIN

"Man is born to die. His works are short-lived. Buildings crumble, monuments decay, and wealth vanishes, but Katahdin in all its glory forever shall remain the mountain of the people of Maine."

—Gov. Percival Baxter

At 5,267 feet, Katahdin is Maine's highest mountain, so it was named appropriately by the Penobscot Indians—the name means "Greatest Mountain." Ownership of Katahdin was given to the state of Maine permanently by Percival Baxter (governor from 1921 to 1925), when he created Baxter State Park.

The mountain's popularity for hikers increased greatly when the Appalachian Trail was completed in 1937—Katahdin is the northern terminus of the AT. Since most AT hikers travel south to north, Katahdin attracts ever-increasing numbers of thru-hikers. In 1991, there were only 359. By 2015, the number had swelled to 2,137.

In order to protect the park's alpine zone and ensure good management of the park's pristine wild nature, the number of hikers allowed on Katahdin's trails per day is limited. Plan ahead and check the park website (*baxterstateparkauthority.com*) to reserve your spot on the mountain and check group size limits, trail conditions, and park closure times. Thru-hikers are required to pick up a Long Distance Hiker Permit Card in person when they reach the park.

HOME OF THE STORM GOD

Among Native Americans, Katahdin was a sacred and fearsome place, and few ventured there. Its peaks were the home of the bird spirit Pamola, god of thunder and protector of the mountain. Among the Penobscot he was said to have the head of a moose, the body of a man, and the feet and wings of an eagle.

The first non-native (and perhaps the first, period) ascent was made in 1804 by surveyors Charles Turner Jr. and Zachary Adley. No one from the party of eleven suffered Pamola's wrath.

Henry David Thoreau climbed it in 1846 and wrote of his experiences in *The Maine Woods*; young Theodore Roosevelt ascended it in 1878; and even Percival Baxter climbed it before he became governor.

KATAHDIN BY THE NUMBERS

⛰ Horseshoe-shaped, open end facing northeast

⛰ 5 separate peaks
  Howe (4,612-ft No. Howe and 4,734-ft So. Howe)
  Hamlin (4,751 ft)
  Baxter (5,267 ft)
  Pamola (4,912 ft)
  South (5,260 ft)

⛰ 9 trails to the summit
  Knife Edge (1.1 mi)
  Abol (3.8 mi)
  Hunt (5.2 mi)
  Helon Taylor (3.2 mi)
  Dudley (1.3 mi)
  Cathedral (1.7 mi)
  Saddle (2.2 mi)
  Hamlin Ridge (1.5 mi)
  Chimney Pond (3.3 mi)

⛰ Timberline varies from 3,500 to 3,800 feet.

YOU HIKED THAT?

Six of Katahdin's nine trail are rated "very strenuous," the highest classification.

- The toughest by far is the Knife Edge, which connects Pamola and Baxter Peaks. It's pretty much what the name implies, a 1.1-mile trail along a narrow ridge. It is covered with sharp granite rocks, is never more than a few feet wide, and has drops of hundreds of feet on both sides. Not for the faint of heart.

- Another "very strenuous" hike is the Abol Trail on the south side of Katahdin. At 3.8 miles, it is the fastest route to Baxter Peak, but that means it's also one of the steepest. It also features the Abol Slide, a half-mile section of scree and loose rock.

- The longest trail is Hunt, part of the last section of the AT, and accessed from the back of the mountain. Its 5.2 miles ramble over streams, waterfalls, and boulders, and it is considered among the most difficult parts of the AT.

- The 1.7-mile Cathedral Trail is one of the steepest trails and involves a lot of scrambling over large rocks. There are three huge granite structures called Cathedrals 1, 2, and 3 that need to be bypassed. Cathedral is not recommended for descending because of the steepness.

5

WATCH FOR YOUR SHIP TO COME IN

It looks like a lighthouse, but don't be fooled; there's no Fresnel lens at the top of the Portland Observatory. There is, however, an unobstructed view of the harbor that once enabled observers to spot the merchandise-laden sailing vessels coming into port.

Built in 1807, the 86-foot-high octagonal wooden tower on Portland's Munjoy Hill, is the last standing historic maritime signal station in the country. Captain Lemuel Moody built the tower as a business venture during the heyday of sail. Before the tower, ships could not be seen entering the harbor until they had rounded Spring Point Ledge and were almost home. Moody realized he could provide a profitable service to ship owners if they knew when their vessels would arrive.

For a $5.00 annual fee, merchants signed up for the service. Using a powerful telescope, from his vantage point 222 feet above sea level, Moody could spot and identify sailing ships while they were still 30 miles out. When he recognized one, he would hoist a flag that identified the vessel for its owner. Flags could be seen from the ocean and the harbor wharfs. During the War of 1812, the observatory was also used as a watch tower.

PORTLAND OBSERVATORY
TIME LINE

1807	Constructed on Munjoy Hill
1923	Closed due to advent of two-way radio,
	later donated to Portland
1939	Restored and reopened by City of Portland
1972	Listed on National Register of Historic Places
1984	Management transferred to Greater Portland Landmarks
1994	Closed again for powder-post beetle infestation and moisture damage
2000	Reopened
2006	Designated a National Historic Landmark and a National Civil Engineering Landmark

The tower stands on a fieldstone base that keeps it steady during storms, and its octagonal shape lessens wind pressure on the sides. Moody's family continued to operate the tower until 1923, when it was rendered obsolete by two-way radio.

The Observatory is open from Memorial Day to Columbus Day, 10 a.m. to 5 p.m. with guided tours available. The only way up is walk the seven flights to the outdoor balcony. On a clear day, besides far out to sea, it's possible to see Mt. Washington in New Hampshire.

HELPFUL SITE

- *portlandlandmarks.org/observatory/*

6

SHOP AT L.L. BEAN

Most every visitor to Maine visits the L.L. Bean flagship store in Freeport at some point—and should. The store has been open at the same site since 1917, although it has grown and morphed into several buildings. Since 1951, it has been open 24 hours a day, seven days a week, originally not for regular shoppers, but for the convenience of its original primary customers, hunters and fishermen. Leon Leonwood Bean, a hunter and fisherman himself, did not want anyone's trip to the remote Maine woods delayed by having to wait to purchase the right fishing rod, trout fly, or camping gear.

The original store has grown to become a 7-acre campus dominating the town center, easily the biggest attraction in Freeport with its parking lots and four different store buildings. The store now sells furniture and household goods as well as clothing and sporting equipment. There's also a coffee shop, two cafes, an aquarium, a trout pond, and a kids' play area.

- Bean boots and canvas totes still made in Maine.

- Nearly half a million pairs of Bean boots sold annually.

- Free shipping to the United States and Canada.

- Store employees live the lifestyle and give firsthand advice on products.

- No-questions-asked return policy.

- Bean boot was adapted for use by the Army and Navy during World War II.

- Oldest and most successful family-owned business in Maine—*Fortune* magazine included L.L. Bean in the top 100 best places to work.

- Fifty different catalogs mailed annually to 170 countries.

- Three million visitors a year to the Freeport store.

- More than $1 billion in annual sales.

HELPFUL SITE

- *llbean.com*

It all started with a boot. L.L. Bean returned from one of his hunting trips with cold, wet feet. Hoping not to relive the experience and to keep others from suffering the same fate, he persuaded a cobbler to stitch leather uppers onto a pair of rubber boots. This was the prototype of what is known colloquially worldwide as "the Bean Boot," although its proper name is The Maine Hunting Shoe.

The iconic Bean Boot is such a part of the company image that a 16.5-foot wood and steel version now stands by the main entrance. It's a popular spot for people to meet in Freeport, since it's so hard to miss, and visitors flock to have their pictures taken next to it. Bean officials say if it was a real boot, it would be a size 410.

SEE A WHALE

Thousands of satisfied customers have watched whales and seabirds from the decks of Maine's whale-watching vessels. There may be little that's more exciting or thrilling than the sight of a whale, up close and immense, blowing its breath within feet of the deck. And if they breach, it's a sight that can't even be imagined and will never be forgotten.

Whales are seasonal and come to the Gulf of Maine to feed between spring and October before heading south to warmer waters to give birth. The species that make the trip include right whales, humpbacks, minkes, and finbacks.

Sometimes the whales don't show up where they are supposed to, and if they do, they may not be in the mood to play or breach for human entertainment. However, many whale-watch tours are available and they have pretty good results because they stay in business!

Popular spots for whale watches range from Lubec to Kennebunk. Other tours leave from Bar Harbor, Boothbay, and Portland.

Those not accustomed to boats, or northern ocean waters, should prepare for the possibility of rough weather (potential seasickness) and cold. Even if it's hot on the dock, it can rapidly become cold and breezy

MAINE'S WHALES

RIGHT: *55 feet and 35 tons*
Called right whales because they were the "right" ones for whalers to catch—they are slow swimmers and float when they are killed. They are endangered, with only about 500 or so left.

HUMPBACK: *50 feet and 40 tons*
Humpbacks are performers. They travel up to 16,000 miles and love to "breach" or leap out of the water, flashing their fluked tails on descent. They have distinctive tail markings that allow scientists to identify and track individual whales.

MINKE: *30 feet and 7 tons*
Minkes are the smallest baleen whale, sometimes traveling alone, but more often in small pods.

FINBACK: *70 feet and 40 tons*
The finback is the second-largest baleen whale after the blue whale. They are also on the endangered species list and are not spotted as frequently off Maine as the humpback.

out on the water. Whale watches, like any ocean-based activity, can be canceled due to particularly bad weather, so prepare for that as well. Check with the tour operator for tips on what to bring and what to expect.

HELPFUL SITES

- *visitmaine.com/things-to-do/outdoors... watching/whale-watching-trips/ odysseywhalewatch.com/whale_watching. html*
- *mainewhales.com*
- *barharborwhales.com*
- *exploremainetoday.com/whale-watching-i n-maine.html*

8

SPOT A MOOSE

You can't spot a moose just anywhere. Only a few states can boast a moose population, and outside of Alaska, Maine has the largest, with roughly 75,000 animals. The moose is Maine's official state animal.

Despite the large population, there's no guarantee you will find one. However, there are times of year and day and regions that are best for moose-watching.

Moose tend to appear more frequently from May through July, then again in fall during mating season, which is also a good time not to get too close to a bull moose. Largely docile, they will charge if they feel threatened, so it's best to keep a good distance. Never get between a mother and her calf. Moose are also more likely to be spotted at dawn or dusk, however they are often spotted in the middle of the day in unlikely places. An adult moose moseyed into a Camden office building one summer day a few years ago—just showed up for work.

They are out and about at night, so when driving in moose territory, slow speeds and high vigilance are strongly suggested. They can weigh up to 1,500 pounds and car collisions with moose are often fatal to the front-seat occupants, as well as the moose.

Although their hoofs make them suited to moving through woods and their swimming abilities allow them to spend time in the water, because of their size they prefer to move around in open

spaces, so they are often spotted trotting along Maine's many logging roads or snow-mobile trails. They are also often seen in marshy places when they are dipping their heads to eat the wet greens.

While anyone can have the good fortune to spot a moose just by chance, a visitor with a short time to spend might fare better by connecting with a tour operator. These moose guides know lots about their subject, including the best places to see them.

Sometimes on a Maine road you might spot a number of cars pulled off to the side with people standing outside of them, all looking in the same direction. If you're in an area that looks moose friendly, you might want to pull over and check what they're watching. It could be a moose.

HELPFUL SITE

- *visitmaine.com/things-to-do/out doors-adventure/wildlife-watching/ moose-watching/*

If you just want to take your chances at seeing one on your own, there are places in Maine better suited to moose-spotting.

Baxter State Park, or on the Golden Road, especially near Abol bridge and the ponds.

Aroostook County: Travel up Route 11 and ask the local folks where the best moose-spotting areas are.

Carrabassett Valley: Visitors report spotting moose on the roads regularly.

Rangeley Lakes: Moose are always near water since they use it to keep cool and for bug relief in the summer.

Jackman: Along Route 201 from the Forks to the Canadian border.

Moosehead Lake: Route 15 between Greenville and Rockwood at sunset, or the back road from Greenville to Shirley.

If you toil and wander, hike and drive, and still manage to miss seeing a moose, go to the L.L. Bean store in Freeport to view a stuffed one.

Or, better yet, head for Scarborough and Len Libby Candies on US Route 1. There, you will see Lenny, the Chocolate Moose. Lenny is life-size, brown of course, and reportedly the world's largest chocolate animal sculpture. He's 8 feet tall and more than 9 feet from nose to tail. The temperature around him must never rise above 70 degrees. His sculptor applied 1,700 pounds of milk chocolate over a wire lathe to make Lenny.

9
GET LOST IN THE DESERT

Yes, Maine has a desert—well, something that *looks* like a desert. It's 40 acres of sand in Freeport, deposited when the ice sheet that covered Maine 11,000 years ago retreated, grinding rocks and soil into glacial silt.

Topsoil covered the silt all over Maine. Forests grew and inhabitants as far back as the Abenaki tribes farmed the fertile soil. In the late 1700s, a farmer named Tuttle failed to rotate his crops sufficiently to replenish the nutrients, then added the extra burden of cattle and sheep to further destroy the topsoil.

The soil began to erode so badly that the glacial silt was revealed—at first just a spot the size of a plate, but eventually 40 acres were laid bare. The sand covered farm equipment and even entire buildings. The Tuttle family abandoned the farm in the early 20th century.

But this is America, where there's always an entrepreneur. A man named Henry Goldrup bought the land and opened it as a tourist attraction starting in 1925.

To be a true desert, the land would have to receive a lot less rain, but the appearance of a desert is enough of an attraction to bring thousands of tourists to the site. Originally people walked the land, but now most visitors take a tram tour that lasts thirty minutes around the perimeter, during which the history and geology of the land is explained.

Scientists say the Desert of Maine is an object lesson for what can happen when the land is not properly cared for. Meanwhile, the Desert has made it into *Ripley's Believe It or Not!* From May to October you can have picnics there, buy bags of mixed dirt and gemstones, and visit a farm museum.

10
WHITEWATER RAFTING

Maine has many rivers and several of them have white water. Anyone wanting the thrill of a ride over such rapids in an air-filled platform with a bunch of like-minded (or screaming and terrified) pals, should head for the wilds of Maine.

Whitewater rafting is generally available April to October, though some places limit it to May to September, and the experience is open to people of all ages and skill sets. Only the most experienced rafters should go without a licensed guide, and then only highly skilled groups should tackle the roughest rapids. No one should try it alone. While the water levels are highest in spring, right after the snow melt and runoff, Maine's rivers always have sufficient water because the levels are controlled by hydropower dams and all the dates when releases occur are announced well in advance.

Maine has the most stringent white-water rafting regulations of any state, and companies offering guided raft trips always provide safety equipment, including required helmets, if you don't have your own. Wet suits are also available for rental.

WHERE TO GO

🐊 The **Kennebec River** is one of the most popular, with 12 miles of white water, starting at Harris Station at Indian Pond, traveling through the Kennebec Gorge, and ending at The Forks. Class II–V.

🐊 The **Penobscot River** run begins with a 2-mile trip through Ripogenus Gorge. Twelve miles after that, it ends at Pock-wockamus Falls. In between can be found rapids known as Cribworks and the Exterminator. The lower and Seboomook River sections are easier and best for younger and less-experienced rafters. Class II–V

🐊 **Dead River** is the longest unbroken stretch of whitewater in the east. Its 16-mile route starts at Grand Falls and ends at The Forks. Class IV and V, not a river to take lightly.

INTERNATIONAL SCALE OF RIVER DIFFICULTY

CLASS I: Easy, no obstacles, small ripples, slow current

CLASS II: Moderate, occasional obstacles, medium current with waves

CLASS III: Difficult, longer rapids with strong, irregular currents

CLASS IV: Very Difficult, steeper, longer with numerous obstacles

CLASS V: Extremely Difficult, large vertical drops, strong hydraulics, very swift, irregular currents in heavily obstructed channels

CLASS VI: Nearly Impossible and Very Dangerous. For teams of experts only, after close study and with all precautions taken.

NOTE: Many rivers have different levels of classes along a route, and those can vary from day to day with the water levels.

Research your trip carefully. Some services offer half-day, relatively easy or half-day, not-so-easy Class V excursions. Most trips take a whole day, but some are longer. Sleep in a tent beside the river, or opt for nicer accommodations in a lodge or B&B. You can arrange your own accommodations, but sleeping at the company's digs is often easier. And remember, you're heading for wild territory, so you can't just drive to the raft site. All companies provide detailed information about transportation.

Guides take every precaution to protect rafters and ensure an enjoyable experience. Who wouldn't want to say they rode a rubber raft through places with names such as Moxie, Big Eddy, Caratunk, Dead Stream Rapids, Nasowadnehnuk Falls, and Big Pocwockamus?

HELPFUL SITES

- *raftmaine.com*
- *neoc.com/white-water-rafting-in-maine/*
- *threeriverswhitewater.com*
- *northcountryrivers.com*

11

CANOE THE ALLAGASH

What's an Allagash? It's a few things, all of them located north of Katahdin deep in the North Maine Woods. There's the 65-mile-long Allagash River. There's also Allagash Stream, Allagash Lake, Allagash Falls, Allagash Village, and Allagash Mountain.

Allagash is most often used to refer to the Allagash Wilderness Waterway, a 92-mile stretch of water that includes lakes, ponds, and the entire Allagash River. It is one of the country's best canoeing experiences. No humans inhabit this remote and pristine region, so it's a true wilderness adventure. This also means it's not a day trip. You should plan carefully and thoroughly, but the reward will be worth it.

A canoe trip down the Allagash is not considered a high-risk venture, so it can be a good family adventure—except for one 9-mile stretch of rips at Chase Rapids, but portage service is available for those wishing to avoid the whitewater. You can do the entire 92 miles or just a portion of it, although waterway access is limited to a few sites. Camping is permitted at designated campsites only, on a first-come, first-serve basis, for parties up to twelve.

There are no stores or service stations in this wilderness area, and you can leave your cell phone at home because there's no coverage. It's the perfect antidote to modern society's noise and dependence on electronics. When you enter the North Maine Woods, there's a one-time Bureau of Parks and Lands access fee of $12 for

WHAT'S IN A NAME?

The meaning of *Allagash* is not perfectly clear, but probably derives from the language of the original Algonquin people who lived here or one of their Wabanaki descendants. It either means "hemlock bark," "bark camp," or "bark cabin lake." Clearly, bark is involved.

DON'T MISS

LOCK DAM, an earthen dam built in 1841.

THE TRAMWAY, a table tramway dating from the early 20th century and used to transport logs.

ALLAGASH FALLS, a 40-foot drop, about 13 miles from where the Allagash joins the St. John River at the Canadian border.

EAGLE LAKE AND UMBAZOOKSUS RAILROAD, an abandoned railway built in 1925 to haul pulpwood. The remains of two steam locomotives stand on the shore of Eagle Lake. The rest of the rail cars are there, too, but are so overgrown they're very hard to find.

nonresidents, $7 for residents. Camping fees are similar at $12 and $6. Another $10 fee gets a ranger to move your canoe to avoid Chase Falls. There are also size restrictions on canoes and kayaks. Unwilling to challenge the waterway on your own? There are at least seven outfitter/guide services available. Much information for planning a trip down the Allagash may be found on the web, but two books will help a lot. Novice campers will benefit from *The Allagash Guide*

by Gil Kilpatrick with its tips on packing, menus, itineraries, and equipment. *The Allagash* by Lew Dietz offers information on the history of the region.

HELPFUL SITE
- *maine.gov/dacf/parks/ park_passes_fees_rules/ aww_rules.shtml*

12

EAT A POTATO

The spud is Maine's biggest agricultural product. Inland and hugging the Canadian border, Aroostook County, or The County, is Maine's largest county and premier agricultural site. In the 1940s, Maine's rich soil yielded the largest potato crop in the nation, dropping to eighth place by 1994.

Farming has dropped off in Maine over the years, but organic farming is now on the increase. In 2015, Maine had 517 organic farms, and one organic grower raises 26 varieties in every color potatoes come in. Despite the decrease from historic levels, Maine still harvests 63,000 acres of potatoes, with sales of around $540,000,000 annually.

HOW TO ENJOY MAINE SPUDS

Eat them

Some frozen French fries and potato chips made from Maine potatoes are produced in Maine (look for the blue State of Maine trademark!).

Or find a retailer selling some of the many-colored varieties of organic Maine potatoes and cook them up yourself. Enjoy them at one of Maine's many farm-to-table restaurants.

Drink them

Less than 1 percent of the world's vodka is made from potatoes these days. However,

Only about 10% of Maine's potatoes go directly to home consumption. The rest go to specialty markets:

45% French fries
25% potato seed
20% potato chips

Maine Distilleries in Freeport produces award-winning small-batch vodka and gin made from Maine potatoes.

Watch them grow

The nine-day Maine Potato Blossom Festival is held each July in Aroostook County, when the breathtaking views of Aroostook's sweeping, sloping potato fields are blooming.

The festival is so popular that more than one has been scheduled in recent years, but all at the same time. The Fort Fairfield festival hosts a Potato Queen pageant, a mashed potato wrestling event, a parade with floats, fireworks, and four nights of music.

Pick your own

A few farms actually allow customers to pick their own potatoes in September.

HELPFUL SITES

- *fortfairfield.org/potatoblossom/about-the-maine-potato-blossom-festival.html*
- *mainepotatoes.com*
- *pickyourown.farm/farms/potato-prod3727/maine-me-r3755/*
- *coldrivervodka.com*

HUMPTY DUMPTY, THE MAINE POTATO CHIP

Founded in Portland in the 1940, Humpty Dumpty is technically no longer a Maine company—it's Canadian. But the chips are still made with Maine potatoes and United States sales are almost entirely in Maine. In addition to plain and common flavors like barbecue, salt & vinegar, and sour cream & onion, Humpty Dumpty can be found in these flavors: Dill Pickle, Lobster Bisque, Cheese & Onion, All Dressed, Smokin' Bacon, and Ketchup.

13

LEARN ABOUT THE GOOD LIFE

Helen and Scott Nearing practically invented the back-to-the-land movement. In the 1970s Maine experienced an influx of young, would-be subsistence farmers, many inspired by the Nearings and their Harborside way of life.

But the Nearings actually began their ascetic lifestyle many years before, starting in Vermont in the 1930s, where they bought a woodlot and a farm and began growing their own food. They built nine stone buildings over a twenty-year period and supported themselves through Scott's occasional lectures and by making and selling maple syrup.

When a ski resort threatened to encroach on their rural existence, the Nearings moved to Harborside, Maine, to begin again. They did not wish merely to be farmers, they chose to make a conscious escape from the capitalistic world. Scott was a noted economist, political activist, college professor, and author of many booklets on peace, economic inequality, feminism, and environmental topics. He also wrote many books, including his 1972 autobiography *Making of a Radical.* Helen was a classically trained musician, twenty-one years his junior.

Scott and Helen also coauthored books, including *Living the Good Life: How to Live Simply and Sanely in a Troubled World* in 1954, which became a guidebook for many who wished to emulate the lifestyle. During the Vietnam War, hundreds of anti-war young people traveled to Maine to hear Scott's anti-war message and study the Nearings' homesteading techniques.

Scott lived to be 100, then ended his life by taking no food for a month and half. Helen documented his choice in her book, *Loving and Leaving the Good Life*. Helen died in a car crash twelve years later when she was 91.

Their Forest Farm homestead is now the Good Life Center, a nonprofit educational and retreat center aimed at perpetuating the Nearing legacy and advocating for simple and sustainable living skills.

Anyone can visit the Good Life Center between late Memorial Day and Columbus Day—check the calendar for days and times. There's a speaker series one night a week throughout the summer, and if you want more than a visit, there's a residency available. This seasonal residency involves staying at Forest Farm, living off the land, gardening, maintenance, guiding tours for visitors, and "combining hand labor and intellectual pursuit."

HELPFUL SITE

- *goodlife.org*

14

WATCH FOR PUFFINS

If not the world's cutest bird, puffins are certainly in the running. Round, black-backed, and white-chested, with wings barely long enough to propel their cannon-ball bodies through the air, they sport large beaks with geometric patterns of red, yellow, orange, and black.

Puffins resemble penguins somewhat, but are actually in the auk family. They swim like penguins too, with those short wings outstretched underwater. Their waterproof feathers keep them warm all winter while they dive up to 200 feet seeking prey such as herring and hake. The birds average 10 inches tall, and their stubby wings can flap up to 400 times a minute—allowing a puffin to reach flying speeds of 55 miles per hour.

Nicknames for puffins include "clown of the sea" and "sea parrot." Their scientific name, *Fratercula arctica*, means "little brother of the north," supposedly because their coloring resembles the dress of certain monks.

Puffin-watching boat tours are available to Machias Seal Island from Cutler in Maine and from Grand Manan Island, New Brunswick. It's the only island where puffin watchers may go ashore, and only about fifteen people are allowed on the island at one time, so booking far ahead is suggested. Regulations are enforced by a Canadian wildlife warden. Landings on the island are often not possible due to weather conditions in the Bay of Fundy, and getting ashore can be difficult any time.

Tours to Eastern Egg Rock leave from Boothbay, New Harbor, and Port Clyde. Some cruises have Audubon specialists on board to give you a more enriching experience. The best times to watch puffins are June and July when they are hatching eggs and feeding chicks. Other islands do not have regular puffin tours.

If you don't want to risk seasickness or a canceled tour due to weather conditions, a visit to Audubon's Project Puffin Visitor Center might be in order. Located at 311 Main Steet in Rockland, Project Puffin has interactive exhibits, videos, lectures, all kinds of information about puffins, and a gift shop.

HELPFUL SITES

- *projectpuffin.audubon.org/*
- *mainebirdingtrail.com*
- *explore.org/videos/player discover-the-puffins-of-seal-island-maine*

Once native to Maine, Atlantic puffins were nearly wiped out by early settlers who over-hunted them for food and feathers. In 1973, the effort to restore puffins began on Eastern Egg Rock. Chicks were transplanted from Newfoundland to man-made burrows on the island and were banded so they could be recognized if they returned to raise chicks of their own. Finally, in 1981 Project Puffin saw its first chick hatched on the island in a century.

From 1984 to 1989, a similar transplant project took place on Seal Island National Wildlife Refuge, and in 1992, the puffins recolonized Seal Island.

Now, Maine is the only state with puffin nesting grounds, with five island populations of puffins: Eastern Egg Rock, Seal Island, Matinicus Rock, Machias Seal Island, and Petit Manan.

15
WITNESS A WHIRLPOOL

The Old Sow is the affectionate name given to the biggest tidal whirlpool in the Western Hemisphere, perhaps because of the pig-like noises it makes when it's churning. A more likely explanation for this whirlpool's name, however, is a mispronunciation by early settlers of the word "sough," which is a draining or sucking sound.

This unusual phenomenon is located off the northeast shore of Moose Island, Eastport, and Deer Island, New Brunswick, Canada. Old Sow is surprisingly slow, since the tides in the area are not. It measures 250 feet across and, oddly, is not usually a navigational hazard unless boat operators are inexperienced.

Small craft are urged to avoid the area when the tide is running, especially in times of high wind and spring tides. It's not just the large funnel itself that's risky, it's also the occasional weird turbulence—a combination of currents and eddies, standing walls of water, and lots of other oddly named smaller spouts and gyres.

Old Sow moves around a bit and it's somewhat unpredictable, sometimes even more active on the outgoing tide, mariners report. It's the result of huge amounts of sea water rushing into a confined space—a 400-foot trench around a 120-foot undersea mount and then into another 350-foot trench. Other ledges on the bottom and countercurrents in the tides, combined with strong winds, all alter Old Sow's activity.

One way to see Old Sow is to take a ferry. All the seasonal ferries from Deer Island get close enough for travelers to see lots of activity.

If you don't want to venture onto the water to witness Old Sow's performance up close, try an on-land viewing from Deer Point in the Deer Island Campground near the ferry landing. You can also see it from Water Street or Clark Street on Moose Island, or from the north end of Dog Island.

HELPFUL SITES

- *downeastcharterboattours.com*
- *oldsowwhirlpool.com*
- *bayoffundy.com/about/old-sow-whirlpool/*

16
PAN FOR GOLD

Get rich! Be a prospector! Relive the Gold Rush. Don't forget your bedroll, ax, and perhaps a donkey…

Or not.

But if you do want to try your hand at panning for gold, you can do it in Maine (the state had a mini-gold rush of its own before the famous 1849 rush in California). Gold has been found in many places in Maine, usually as a by-product of other kinds of mining. The amount of the precious metal that's been found has never been spectacular, so you shouldn't plan on striking the mother lode.

Western Maine is the prime area for finding gold and the best spot is the Swift River, a tributary of the Androscoggin. Prospectors often try the major tributaries such as Berdeen Stream, and the East and West branches of the Swift. If you're willing to do a bit of hiking to remote areas, try Tumbledown Brook, West Brook, and some

other drainages around Webb Lake in Weld. The Sandy River, a 73-mile long tributary in Franklin County, drains into the Kennebec River. It's another waterway where gold has been found in the river and its tributaries. Try Chandler Mill and Crossman Streams near Madrid. Also in Franklin County, there's the Nile Brook in Rangeley.

The Kennabago River in Oxford County is another spot to try. Nearby Cupsuptic River was once closed due to riverbank erosion caused by gold-panners, some of whom used banned mechanized equipment. Check for updates.

Over in Somerset County, try the aptly named Gold Brook, which runs through Bowman in Oxford County, Chain of Ponds in Franklin County, and Chase Stream and Appleton Township in Somerset County. Also in Somerset, take a chance on the South Branch of the Penobscot River near the Quebec border, which flows through

Canada Falls Lake and Seboomook Lake.

Midsummer is considered the best time for panning—the weather is warm and the water is usually low. Check the Maine government site for regulations and suggestions. There are also businesses who will offer instruction, rental of panning equipment, and guidance to panning areas.

Materials for gold-hunting are fairly simple and easy to find. They're for sale online for one thing, and general stores near popular Maine gold-panning areas have many essentials a would-be prospector needs.

Remember that what you find may be merely specks of gold, so it's important to learn the proper technique and have adequate equipment to separate fine gold from sand and gravel. Nuggets may be found, but they're rare in Maine. No special permits are needed as long as you use unmechanized equipment, but check with the state for any possible changes. Landowner permission is needed on private land, of course.

HELPFUL SITE

- *https://www1.maine.gov/dacf/mgs/ explore/minerals/guide/maps/swift.pdf*

17

BUILD A BOAT

Maine's miles of forest once made the state a premier center for boatbuilding in the days of sail. While fiberglass and other materials have largely replaced wood, the craft of wooden boatbuilding is not dead. Some boatbuilders still make classic wooden boats, and there are a few schools available to train anyone interested in learning the skill.

Wooden Boat School in Brooklin offers classes ranging from the simplest basics for beginners to more complicated classes for experienced builders. There are a number of options available for students to work on, from small models to dories. Open nearly forty years, the school's courses are available from June through September and include techniques for restoring wooden boats as well.

The Apprenticeship in Rockland is a nonprofit school that offers an intensive two-year apprenticeship program to teach all aspects of wooden boatbuilding, a shorter, twelve-week course focused on building a 12-foot boat, and an Extended/Advanced Intensive Program for students who have some experience.

Sailing classes are an important part of the Apprenticeshop's mission and are offered during spring, summer, and fall in Rockland Harbor. Various short courses and workshops are offered throughout the year in areas such as kayak construction or half-hull model building. The school also partners with the local high school's Fisherman's Academy, and offers a girls-only workshop led by a woman instructor.

The Boat School, the oldest boatbuilding program in the country, evolved from a local vo-tech institute in Eastport to a community college and is now becoming a public/private educational center. The school offers wooden boatbuilding courses as well as classes in composite boatbuilding, mechanics, rigging, boat repair and restoration, and more. It's a more industry-driven curriculum, where students can earn certification as a composites technician.

At the other end of the coast, *The Landing School* in Kennebunk offers wooden boatbuilding, composite boatbuilding, yacht design, and courses in marine systems. Like the Boat School, The Landing School is career-oriented, with courses leading to diplomas or degrees, but also offers short summer courses, including "boot camps" on particular topics and a captains course. Students range from high school graduates to adults seeking career changes.

HELPFUL SITES
- *thewoodenboatschool.com/index.php*
- *apprenticeshop.org*
- *theboatschool.net/aboutus.html*
- *landingschool.edu*

18

RUN THE BEACH TO BEACON

Started by Maine's own famous runner, Joan Benoit Samuelson, winner of the first women's Olympic marathon in 1984, the Beach to Beacon 10K is the largest in the state, attracting top-flight runners from around the world.

Taking place on the first Saturday in August, the race begins at Crescent Beach State Park in Cape Elizabeth, birthplace and home of Samuelson. After 6.2 miles of ocean-side beauty, more than 6,500 runners end up at Fort Williams, next to Portland Head Light—the country's most photographed lighthouse.

Runners range from world-class champions to rank amateurs, but spots are limited. The race is so popular that when online registration opens in March, the slots are sold out within minutes. If you wish to participate, plan ahead and sit by the computer awaiting the brief window of opportunity. Besides the main attraction, other races are offered including a 1-mile high school race and a kids Fun Run.

Since 1997, the Beach to Beacon has awarded prizes to winners in different categories and raised money for charity. According to Samuelson, the race is about celebrating health and fitness, as well as providing an opportunity to give back to the community.

HELPFUL SITE

• beach2beacon.org/

Can't get a spot? Perhaps you'd be content to join the thousands of spectators who watch the race Or you could be one of more than 800 volunteers helping out. You can sign up online.

If the competition for a spot in the race is too nerve-wracking, you can run the race in the privacy of home on your own treadmill. Download a free app with the virtual race course to your iPad, put the iPad on your treadmill, and go. You can also purchase the entire 10K course filmed from a runner's point of view on race day. Use the purchased version of the app to re-experience your own race, compete with friends, or train for your next Beach to Beacon.

19

GO MUSHING

Maine averages 200 inches of snow in winter, and skiing, snowshoeing, and snowmobiling are popular activities, but if you're looking for something different—try dogsledding.

Mushing isn't for everyone, but if you want the experience of riding behind a team of eager, well-trained dogs through a snowy forest or across a frozen lake, you can find it in Maine.

Kennels in western Maine and areas around Baxter, Bethel, and beyond offer dogsledding adventures that range from a one-hour ride to several days of back-country sledding (not for the faint of heart). Some offer night rides and some specialize in speed.

If you decide to go, check carefully the list of clothing and accessories you will need to ensure a safe, frostbite-free experience. You will learn the commands that tell the dogs where to turn and when to stop or go. You may not finish ready to take on the Iditerod, but you might be ready to take on the old TV role of Sgt. Preston of the Yukon.

THE CAN-AM CROWN

If you're more interested in watching than participating, there's the Maine version of the Iditerod, the Can-Am Crown International Sled Dog Race. It's held every year in late winter, usually to coincide with the Iditerod. The 250-mile course begins in Fort Kent and competitors often go on to vie in the Iditerod. *can-am-crown.net*

HELPFUL SITES

- *visitmaine.com/things-to-do/out doors-adventure/winter-activities/ dog-sledding/*
- *ultimatedogsleddingexperience.com*
- *mainewoodsdiscovery.com/ dog-sled-adventure/*

20

DIG FOR TREASURE

Want to search for tourmaline, several varieties of quartz, topaz, or beryl? Grab a sturdy rock hammer, some small shovels, chisels, gloves, and safety glasses, and hit the road for a likely spot. Many rockhounds head first for the Mt. Mica area in Paris the first mine in Paris Hill, which is still producing.

Mt. Mica was named and mined primarily for the huge quantities of mica found there, a substance that was in great demand for industrial uses. Tourmaline and other gems were found along with the mica, and gems were dug there until the 1970s. In 2003, new owners of the mine decided to dig deeper into the pegmatite, an igneous rock that is a coarsely crystalline type of granite where most Maine gems are found. Their decision paid off: They have made some of the best finds of multi-colored tourmaline specimens since the mine opened in the 19th century.

The area in Maine where feldspar and mica were mined remains one of the best spots to find tourmaline, beryl, quartz, and amethyst. Besides these, pegmatite deposits also have produced chrysoberyl, lepidolite, and spodumene. Metamorphic rocks have produced some garnet, kyanite, andalusite, sodalite, and staurolite. Dozens of old feldspar and mica mines are scattered across parts of Androscoggin, Sagadahoc, and especially the southern half of Oxford County.

Some mining spots that have traditionally been open may close to the public suddenly, so it's best to check out any site before traveling there. Permission must be requested from landowners to use any private property.

Maine has a few businesses that offer guided mining experiences for a fee. If you just want to look at Maine gemstones, many are on display in the Maine State Museum in Augusta.

FIRST IN THE NATION

The first gemstone mine in the United States was started in Paris, Maine, in 1821, completely by accident. Friends Elijah Hamlin and Ezekiel Holmes went for a hike and Hamlin spotted a shiny green crystal under the roots of a fallen tree. A Yale professor identified the crystal as tourmaline—the most valuable mineral or semi-precious gem found in the state, and Maine's official mineral. The Hamlin necklace, made of fine tourmalines from the mine, is in the collection of the Harvard University Mineralogical Museum.

HELPFUL SITES

- *digmainegems.com/*
- *maine.gov/dacf/mgs/explore/minerals/ facts/mincolec.htm*
- *goldrushnuggets.com/rageandmiinm.html*
- *mainemineralmuseum.org*

21

CATCH A MOVIE AT THE DRIVE-IN

Remember those lazy, hazy, crazy days of summer when everyone piled into a car and headed to the drive-in? Revisit those days with a trip to one of Maine's outdoor movie screens. They're probably considered retro now, but they've been here all along. Maine is one of only fifteen states that still has one of these distinctly American institutions. At

The Bridgton Twin Drive-In (383 Portland Rd.) offers two choices of double features on its two screens. Open seven days a week in summer, rain or shine, Bridgton screens retro movies on Tuesdays. Snack food is available.

Skowhegan Drive-In (201 Waterville Rd.) Another 1950s-era drive-in, Skowhegan offers single showings and double features. Open seven days a week, rain or shine. Food available. Charges per person, cash only.

Prides Corner Drive-In (651 Bridgton Rd., Westbrook) This family-owned theater has been open since 1953. There is a snack bar.

Bangor Drive-In (1674 Hammond St. Hermon) Reopened after a thirty-year hiatus, this twin-screen outdoor cinema shows double features of first-run movies. Snack bar. Charges by the carload.

Skylite Drive-In (11th Ave., Madawaska) The single screen has single showings only. Rates are per person, and the snack bar features dough boys.

last count, only 348 drive-ins in the country were still working. Maine has six of them.

The Saco Drive-In (969 Portland Rd.) offers a double feature—prices vary by the number of people in the car (up to five)—and "casual food" of the pizza slice, hot dog, burger, and chicken nugget variety is available.

22

GO TO THE PARK

The national park that is. Acadia National Park—located mostly on Mount Desert Island, a big chunk of Isle au Haut, a little on Baker Island, and a portion of the Schoodic Peninsula—is the ninth most visited national park in the United States The 47,000-acre park contains many spectacular sights, including the tallest mountain on the East Coast, wild scenic views, cliffs, wildlife, gardens, Thunder Hole, a museum, and a restaurant overlooking a pond.

A variety of travel methods will get you to the views. There are 45 miles of carriage roads that allow for bicycles, hikers, horses, and (rarely these days) carriages. Some restrictions apply on pets, horses, and bicycles on some of the roads. The most popular road is the Park Loop Road, which, as its name suggests, loops the park with stops at all the popular points of interest. There are also numerous hiking trails within the park, with varying distances and difficulty levels.

THINGS TO CHECK OUT

Cadillac Mountain: Where you can see more than 100 miles to Mt. Katahdin in the north and Nova Scotia in the east.

Sand Beach: One of the few true sand beaches this far north in Maine. Swim only if you dare, as the water rarely exceeds 55 degrees.

Little Hunters Beach: The smooth rounded cobbles make the ocean sing as it washes in and out over the stones.

Otter Cliff: 110 vertical feet of stunning pink Cadillac granite.

Thunder Hole: When the waves are right they make a booming noise and spout water up to 40 feet.

Jordan Pond House: The only restaurant in the park is famous for its popovers, chowder, and a great view of Jordan Pond.

Schoodic: This is on the quiet side, with staggering views of the rugged coast.

HELPFUL SITE

nps.gov/acad/planyourvisit/index.htm

23

SAIL ON A WINDJAMMER

It all started with Captain Frank Swift in 1936. Steamships had ended the golden age of sail and Swift hated to see the graceful schooners disappear. He figured one way to save these beautiful vessels was to interest people in becoming passengers for a cruise along Maine's scenic coast. The word "windjammer" was originally a derogatory term used by steamship captains, but Swift's business changed the meaning completely.

His "windjammer" business worked, and by the 1950s other captains joined the effort. When Swift retired in 1961, he left a flourishing industry that has spread to ports beyond Camden, including Rockland, Boothbay, and Bar Harbor.

The schooners vary in size, which limits the number of guests. Accommodations vary as well. The duration of trips ranges from a short two-hour harbor cruise to one night or even a week. Some vessels may be chartered for a group sail.

Part of the charm of a windjammer cruise is the opportunity to help with the work on board—hoisting sales, swabbing decks, anything that needs doing—or not. Choose a cruise to coincide with the events centered around the windjammers, such as Windjammer Days in late June, the Great Schooner Race in early July, the Windjammer Parade in mid-July, or others.

Often passengers will get to enjoy a real Maine clam/lobster

Many of the sailing vessels in the fleet are venerable craft, some designated as official national treasures, while a few were built exclusively for the business. A few notable vessels that have graced the fleet over the years include the *Adventure*, one of the last two existing Gloucester fishing schooners, now restored and residing in Gloucester again; and the *Bowdoin*, built in Maine for Admiral MacMillan's Arctic explorations, and now serving as Maine's official vessel at Maine Maritime Academy in Castine.

bake during a cruise—maybe even on an uninhabited island. Sometimes the vessel will drop anchor in a quiet cove with no houses in view (this is still possible in Maine) and passengers can usually go ashore to explore. Seeing a whale is not guaranteed, but often happens. However, there's no doubt passengers will see osprey, bald eagles, and many other sea birds, as well as seals and porpoises.

The season begins in June and ends in September. There are specialty cruises catering to a wide range of interests, including beer-tasting, chocolate-tasting, photography, pirate adventures, lighthouse cruises, storytelling/humor cruises, and whale-watching.

HELPFUL SITES

- *sailmainecoast.com*
- *mainewindjammercruises.com*
- *visitmaine.net/page/57/windjammers*

24

MAKE MAPLE SYRUP

All you need are some buckets, several sugar maple trees, a big pan for boiling the sap, and patience, lots of patience.

It takes about ten gallons of sap to produce a single quart of maple syrup, but is there much sense going to all the trouble for less than a gallon? The University of Maine Extension Service offers directions for tapping trees and collecting and boiling down the sap. Any maple tree will work, but sugar maples work best. Sugar content also varies from tree to tree, or by time of day.

Anyone lacking the time or trees to create their own maple syrup can do the next best thing: Visit one of more than five dozen sugarhouses on Maine Maple Sunday, the fourth Sunday in March (many are also open that Saturday) to see a demonstration of how maple syrup is made, try syrup samples, and enjoy other activities. Syrup and other maple goodies will most certainly be available for purchase at the sugarhouses.

The identity of the person who discovered how to make maple syrup is lost to history (most likely it was passed on to European settlers by the Indians), but according to the extension website, in 1663, English chemist Robert Boyle told colleagues in Europe, "There is in some parts of New England a kind of tree whose juice that weeps out its incision, if it is permitted slowly to exhale away the superfluous moisture, doth congeal into a sweet and saccharin substance."

While there is no better substance known to man for pouring over pancakes and waffles, maple syrup also makes a wonderful topping for ice cream, an ingredient in many delicious sauces such as barbecue sauce, and an alternative sweetener in baked goods and baked beans. Plus, there's maple candy. You can make your own maple candy by boiling down syrup—and you don't even have to make the syrup yourself.

HELPFUL SITE

- *extension.umaine.edu/publications/7036e/ mainemapleproducers.com/maine-maple-sunday-map.html*

25

DISCOVER AMERICA'S FIRST FORT KNOX

The Fort Knox that's famous for gold bullion, and that's an active Army base...that's not our Fort Knox. That one's in Kentucky.

Maine's Fort Knox is the first one, built in Prospect, on the narrows of the Penobscot River in the mid-1800s. It was constructed to defend the river from another British invasion. Eastern Maine had been attacked and defeated by the British in both land and naval battles during the Revolutionary War and the War of 1812.

Designed in the shape of a pentagon, with the capacity for more than 130 cannons, the fort's armaments were aimed at both sides of the river. Despite a lengthy construction period, the fort was never

really completed, nor did it ever fire a shot at an enemy. It was manned during wars until 1923, when it was sold to the state for $2,121. Besides being a Maine State Historic Site, it is also a United States National Historic Landmark.

Fort Knox is one of the best-preserved old forts on the New England coast. You can access the grounds year-round, but the Visitor and Education Center is only open May to October. Entrance fees help the Friends of Fort Knox maintain the buildings. It is located next to the Penobscot Narrows Bridge and Observatory (#43). Entrance may be purchased for the fort alone, or for both.

HELPFUL SITES

- *http://fortknox.maineguide.com/*
  northamericanforts.com/East/me.html

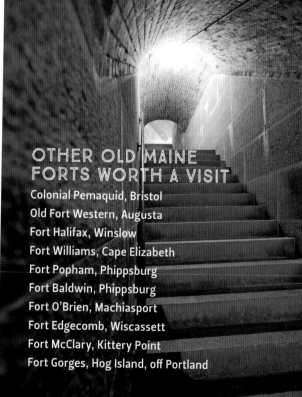

OTHER OLD MAINE FORTS WORTH A VISIT

Colonial Pemaquid, Bristol
Old Fort Western, Augusta
Fort Halifax, Winslow
Fort Williams, Cape Elizabeth
Fort Popham, Phippsburg
Fort Baldwin, Phippsburg
Fort O'Brien, Machiasport
Fort Edgecomb, Wiscassett
Fort McClary, Kittery Point
Fort Gorges, Hog Island, off Portland

26
CATCH A LOBSTER

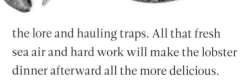

Maine's number 1 fishery provides the favorite dish of summer travelers. Many say lobster just tastes better when eaten beside the sea on a beautiful summer day. But most say it's fabulous anywhere, any time. So while you're in Maine, cook it, eat it, bring home souvenirs emblazoned with it, and perhaps even catch one yourself.

Lobster fishing is a tradition in Maine, which lands around 80 percent of *all* lobster caught in the United States. Drive the coast, visit an island, or poke down any peninsula and you won't have to look far to see the signs of lobster culture—boats bobbing in harbors; piles of colorful traps stacked in dooryards; signs for lobster pounds and lobster co-ops.

DO IT YOURSELF
Besides eating lobster in Maine, in some ports you can buy a ticket on a lobster boat and enjoy the experience of lobstering, learning the lore and hauling traps. All that fresh sea air and hard work will make the lobster dinner afterward all the more delicious.

GO TO THE RACES
Don't want to work for your supper? How about watching those high-powered lobster boats race against each other? There are a number of lobster boat races each summer. Schedules vary year to year, so check online.

HYPNOTIZE A LOBSTER

If you cozy up to a lobsterman, ask if he knows how to hypnotize a lobster. You could try it yourself — stand it on its head and rub between the eyes with your finger for a minute or so. The lobster should remain standing on its head without support. We don't recommend it.

HELPFUL SITES
- *maineoceanadventures.com/ casco-bay-tours/maine-lobstering-tour/ lobstertrail.com*
- *catch-cook-your-own-lobster/ luckycatch.com*
- *maine-lylobster.com*
- *mainelobsterfestival.com*

POOR MAN'S FOOD

Hard to believe now, but in colonial days lobster was so plentiful it was considered trash food, good only to feed Indians and the poor.

WHAT'S IN A NAME?

Commonly referred to as "the Champagne of Maine" (Allen's even uses this term on their website), the standard sombrero mixture has taken on a range of monikers:

- Fat Ass in a Glass
- Gorilla Juice
- Bitch Whiskey
- Trailer Park Toddy
- Biddeford Martini
- Double Wide

And then there are the cocktail alternatives to the sombrero:

- Burnt Trailer: one part Allen's, two parts Moxie
- The Service: a shot each of Allen's, Santa Maria Al Monte, and espresso
- Block Island Iced Tea: equal parts Allen's, vanilla vodka, and hazelnut liqueur

27

GET TIPSY ON ALLEN'S COFFEE BRANDY

As the name implies, Allen's is an alcoholic beverage. It's the number 1 selling alcoholic beverage in the state. In fact, it accounts for four of the top ten-selling alcoholic beverages by bottle. How is that possible? It comes in four different sizes. Allen's routinely sells 98,000 cases, or a million bottles annually. It's not even made in Maine, but in Massachusetts, but most of it is sold here. It's truly Maine and the unofficial state alcoholic beverage.

Sweet, coffee-flavored, and 60 proof, Allen's is an interesting combination of a drink that's genuinely popular with many people, but also serves as an ironic joke for others. Ordering a sombrero, a "brandy drink," or just an "Allen's" in Maine will likely get you the most popular form, Allen's and milk over ice.

Try it. You might not like it, but you will have sampled a piece of Maine. Like whoopie pies, once unknown outside the region but now nearly ubiquitous, Allen's has been spotted on the cocktail menus of upscale Boston and Manhattan bistros. What next?

HELPFUL SITES
- *allenscoffeebrandy.com*
- *punchdrink.com/articles the-champagne-of-maine-allens-invades-the-cocktail-bar/*

28

VISIT THE SHAKERS

Sabbathday Lake, Maine, is home to the last remaining Shaker community in the world, with only two remaining members, but a wealth of information and products to share with the public.

Shakerism once spread throughout the east from Maine to Kentucky. At its peak, there were 4,000 to 6,000 members in 23 United States communities. Now the 1,800-acre, eighteen-building Sabbathday Lake community in New Gloucester is the last one standing.

The nonprofit group Friends of the Shakers helps out around the farm, with its members traveling from around the world to get the community ready for winter or to help spruce up the grounds for summer. The group also raises money to preserve the buildings and land. And they welcome volunteers if you want to help out.

The Shakers derive income from the farm, including a large apple orchard, and still produce some small woodenware, baskets, yarn, weavings, food, art, and specialty items such as made-to-order "food stones." The Shakers never shunned technology, so you can shop the Shaker store online.

The Sabbathday Lake community is open to the public from May to October. Tours of the museum are available by advance reservation. Several one-hour guided tours of the Shaker Village are available from Memorial Day to Columbus Day. A tour of the herb garden is included with the guided tour or may be purchased separately. The Sunday service is also open to the public. Scholars and authors can explore the collection and library with an appointment. There are also musical events held throughout the season.

The Shakers are Christians who base their beliefs on celibacy, community, and pacifism. Founded in 1747 in England, the original name of the breakaway Quaker sect is United Society of Believers in Christ's Second Appearing. Founder Mother Ann Lee fled to America with eight followers to escape persecution after being imprisoned for her beliefs.

Shakers are noted for their beautiful furniture and their inventiveness—the flat broom, circular saw blade, spring clothespin, paper seed envelope, a wheel-driven washing machine, a threshing machine, and a new type of fire engine are all Shaker creations.

HELPFUL SITES

- *maineshakers.com*
- *friendsoftheshakers.org*
- *maineshakers.com/shop/*

94

29

ENJOY ONE OF THE SWEETER THINGS

A few years back the whoopie pie lost out to the blueberry pie as the state's official dessert in the Maine legislature and was relegated to being the official Maine treat.

Blueberry pies are wonderful of course, but they are also fairly common in other places, while the whoopie pie—not really a pie at all—is considered a Maine invention. Pennsylvania might disagree—they think they invented it, while food historians suspect it was likely first made in a Boston bakery. Wherever it was made, it was nurtured in Maine and has become part of the culture here. You can find them in just about any store, shop, or gas station that sells food of any kind. Many small and a few large bakeries make and sell whoopie pies by the millions in stores and restaurants around the country.

Although the traditional whoopie pie

Ship me Worldwide
WhoopiePies.com

Maine can boast the first-ever shop in the world devoted exclusively to whoopie pies. Wicked Whoopies has two locations, in Farmingdale and Freeport, and sells pies by Amy Bouchard—Maine's Whoopie Pie Queen. Bouchard made the World's Largest Whoopie Pie in 2011 at the Maine Mall, tipping the scales at just over 1,000 pounds.

is considered to be two dark chocolate cakes shaped like hamburger buns with a white filling (ingredients arguable) similar to buttercream and often (but not always) containing Marshmallow Fluff, they are now made and sold in a variety of flavors. So could you get around the official treat designation by making a blueberry whoopie pie? We're not sure it's been done yet.

HELPFUL SITES

- *wickedwhoopies.com*
- *mainewhoopiepiefestival.com*

30

SOAR IN A HOT-AIR BALLOON

Maine may not be the first place that pops into your mind when you think of hot-air balloons, but remember, both hot-air and helium balloon trips to set Atlantic crossing records have started in Maine.

Maine has two festivals to help you discover a love of ballooning. Since 2003, Presque Isle has hosted the Crown of Maine Balloon Fest for four days in late August, when hot-air balloon owners from the United States and Canada celebrate the world's oldest form of air travel. Just before dawn and just before sunset (6 a.m. and 6 p.m.), the balloons carry passengers over vast stretches of Aroostook's fields and valleys, usually landing on someone's farm.

The Great Falls Balloon Festival takes place over three days in mid- to late August at Simard-Payne Memorial Park in Lewiston. This festival has been running since 1992, and attracts approximately 100,000 visitors to Maine's second most populous urban area. Usually there are five launches, also at 6 a.m. and 6 p.m., available to would-be riders. There are also balloons that can accommodate larger groups of up to ten passengers. Both festivals end balloon rides with a traditional champagne toast.

So if you want to spend an hour imagining yourself as Phileas Fogg in *Around the World in 80 Days*, or just want a new, mostly silent, view of wonderful Maine scenery from aloft, a hot-air balloon ride might be just the thing. If the festivals' timing doesn't work, there are at least three companies throughout the state that offer balloon rides.

ACROSS THE SEA

The helium-filled *Double Eagle II*, the first balloon ever to cross the Atlantic, launched from Presque Isle and landed in Miserey, France, on August 17, 1978.

In 1984, Joe W. Kittinger left Caribou in his helium-filled balloon, *Rosie O'Grady's Balloon of Peace*, and completed the first solo trans-atlantic balloon flight, landing in Savona, Italy.

Richard Branson and Per Lindstand made the first successful hot-air balloon transatlantic crossing in 1987 in their *Virgin Atlantic Flyer*, launching from Sugarloaf Mountain and flying to Ireland.

HELPFUL SITES

- *crownofmaineballoonfest.org*
- *greatfallsballoonfestival.org*
- *hotfunballoons.com*
- *maineballooning.com*

31

DRIVE ROUTE 1 FROM KITTERY TO FORT KENT

Route 1 through Maine is the second-longest stretch of this longest north–south highway in the United States. The longest stretch is in Florida, at the other end of the 2,390-mile road, but only by 4 miles.

Driving it in Maine is easy, although it will take some time to do it right. You could, of course, just drive straight through the 529 miles, and be done in a long day. But where's the fun in that?

Take your time, stop overnight, and experience much if not most of Maine's various geographic treats, from the peaks and valleys of agricultural Aroostook County, to the entire coast. While en route, take in a few of the unnatural attractions as well.

Starting from Kittery at the bottom, Route 1 snakes through every little coastal

village. They're all pretty full of visitors and traffic during summer, so you might as well stop and visit the art galleries, boutiques, and gift shops, and perhaps eat a lobster roll. You might even stretch your legs and take a walk on the beach.

Route 1 ends (or begins) in Fort Kent, with several signs to mark it. One reads, "This site marks the Northern terminus of Historic United States Rt. 1, originating in Key West, Florida." The back side of the same sign reads, "This marks the beginning of United States Rt. 1, ending in Key West, Florida, 2209 miles South." Another says simply, "America's First Mile."

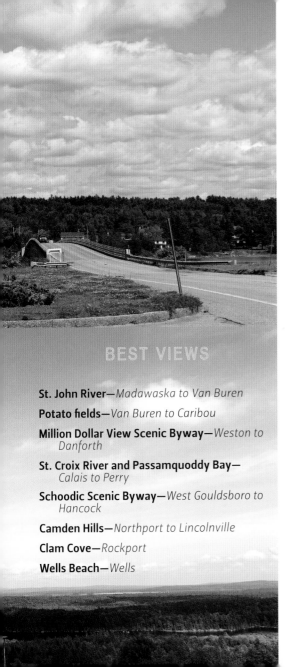

BEST VIEWS

St. John River—*Madawaska to Van Buren*

Potato fields—*Van Buren to Caribou*

Million Dollar View Scenic Byway—*Weston to Danforth*

St. Croix River and Passamquoddy Bay—*Calais to Perry*

Schoodic Scenic Byway—*West Gouldsboro to Hancock*

Camden Hills—*Northport to Lincolnville*

Clam Cove—*Rockport*

Wells Beach—*Wells*

MAINE ROUTE 1
BY THE NUMBERS

21 McDonald's restaurants

96 churches

1 wind farm

4 degree-granting colleges

28 cemeteries

4 border crossings

25 self-storage facilities

3 auction houses

2 islands

2 hubcap yards

8 moose crossing signs

41 Irving stations

58 car dealerships

14 Family Dollar stores

5 Grange halls

1 purple house

2 state parks

3 stop signs (actual signs, not stop lights)

32

DECK THE WALLS WITH ART

The Portland Museum of Art, Maine's oldest art institution, houses a collection of more than 18,000 pieces of American, European, and contemporary art, as well as many works by Maine artists. The collection includes paintings, pottery, porcelain, furniture, and sculpture.

The PMA also owns and operates the studio of marine and coastal painter Winslow Homer on the rocky coast at Prouts Neck. Art historians generally agree that Homer didn't reach his true artistic maturity until he came to Maine. His studio was declared a National Landmark in 1966. The PMA bought and restored it in 2006 and now opens the studio for guided tours.

Located in the heart of the arts district downtown, the main PMA building—the modern, award-winning Charles Shipman Payson Building, was opened in 1983. Besides the Homer studio and the Payson building, the PMA owns and displays art in an 1801 Federal three-story mansion known as the McLellan House and in the 1911 Beaux Arts-style L.D.M. Sweat Memorial Galleries.

HELPFUL SITES

- *portlandmuseum.org*
- *creativeportland.com/arts/first-friday-art-walk/*
- *maineartmuseums.org*

FIRST FRIDAY ART WALK

Portland truly has a dynamic arts scene, and there's no better way to experience it than on a First Friday Art Walk. On the first Friday of each month, galleries and museums open their doors to the public. Artists show off their work and there are public concerts and film screenings—and it's all free.

THE MAINE ART TRAIL

Beyond Portland, Maine is bursting with art museums and galleries. If you love art you can follow the Maine Art Museum Trail for 200 miles from Ogunquit to Bangor, with inland forays to Waterville and Lewiston, and at least one island excursion to Monhegan. The trail promises the opportunity to see 73,000 works of art and "infinite possibilities."

33

EAT BEAN HOLE BEANS

As with many old New England tradi-tions, it's becoming more difficult to find authentic bean hole beans in Maine. How-ever, with diligence and good timing, it can be done. Or, you can do it yourself.

Like a traditional shore-side lobster bake, bean hole beans are cooked in a pit lined with stone. First dig a 3-foot-deep hole, line it with stones, and build a roar-ing fire that burns until it turns into a hot bed of coals. Then lower a covered pot (cast iron is best) into the pit, cover with some of the coals, then cover it in dirt and leave it to cook all day or even overnight—at least eight hours.

Obviously, this means you'll have to start working on the beans the day before, with a shovel, a pile of good hardwood, and a bunch of rocks. Some say the rocks can be left out if you've made enough coals. Some

say the pot should rest in the coals, and the hot stones (if used) placed on the lid to pro-vide heat and keep the dirt off. As with most things, you'll have to decide through trial and error which method works best for you.

Recipes vary, too, as much as recipes for "Grandma's Apple Pie." You can use just about any kind of bean, from Maine Soldier Beans, to Yellow Eye, Great Northern, or Jacob's Cattle, but they must be parboiled before taking them to the bean hole. A proper cast-iron bean pot is fat and has three legs, a handle, and a really tight-fitting lid. Use heavy pot holders or mitts to remove the pot from the pit because the handle will be HOT.

Recipes for bean hole beans are plen-tiful online. A Google search will give you pages of results, including a recipe on the *New York Times* and video directions on YouTube.

WHO THOUGHT THIS UP?

The first settlers in New England learned about bean hole beans from Native Americans. The Penobscot cooked their beans in clay pots with bits of venison and flavored them with maple syrup. The settlers later switched to salt pork and molasses. The beans became a favorite at lumber camps when Maine's industry was at its peak and continued as a tradition for community suppers throughout the state.

WHERE TO EAT 'EM

Rangeley Lakes Logging Museum Festival Days, late July. *maineforestrymuseum.org*

Maine Forest and Logging Museum offers bean hole beans on two days as a noon meal, one in early August at their Heavy Metal event and one in early October during Living History Days. *maineforestandloggingmuseum.org*

Harpswell Scout Association's annual bean hole supper fundraiser, usually on the first Saturday in August. *facebook.com/harpswellneighbors/*

The **Patten Lumbermen's Museum**'s Annual Bean-Hole Bean Dinner, always the second Saturday in August. *lumbermensmuseum.org/events-3/*

Folk Arts Area at the **Common Ground Country Fair**, always the third weekend after Labor Day, around noon on each day of the fair. *mofga.org/Publications/MaineOrganicFarmerGardener/Winter20062007/CommonGroundsBeanHole-Beans/tabid/659/Default.aspx*

Fryeburg Fair, served Tuesday, Thursday, and Saturday during the first week in October, 1 p.m. at the Fryeburg Fair Farm Museum. *fryeburgfair.org/Events-Attractions/Points-of-Interest/Museum*

34
MAKE THE MOST OF MONHEGAN

Maine claims approximately 4,600 islands, including a few located inland on lakes. While Mount Desert is technically an island, most visitors think of it only as Acadia and don't much consider it as an island. Monhegan on the other hand… retains its indelible island-ness in our hearts and minds.

First visited by Europeans in 1614, Monhegan was already known to Native Americans as prime fishing ground. Today, a few island residents earn their living lobstering, but tourism forms the backbone of the economy. Rugged, remote, impeccably beautiful, Monhegan has drawn artists and other visitors for more than a hundred years. With its slower pace—you can only get there by boat and there are no cars or paved roads—and stunning natural environment, Monhegan provides a heady respite from everyday life.

Only about a square mile in area, Monhegan has some 12 miles of hiking trails passing through forests, over cliffs, and along beaches. Islanders and visitors alike work to preserve the wild nature of the island and there's an island lighthouse, a museum of art and history, and a library to preserve the cultural history of the island.

There are a number of inns and cottages, including the legendary Monhegan House and The Island Inn. For efficiency and water-use concerns, some places only have communal bathrooms. Three boats can get you there, leaving from Port Clyde,

New Harbor, and Boothbay Harbor. They usually make daily runs in the summer, but fewer in winter.

Monhegan retains its strong attraction to artists and it's not uncommon to spot an easel with a painter re=creating some iconic scene. Many resident artists have galleries or open studios where you can see and purchase their work. Of course you don't have to be an artist to enjoy Monhegan. You just need a sense of adventure.

HELPFUL SITE

- *monheganwelcome.com/*

THINGS TO SEE

Swim Beach	Ice Pond
Manana Island	Lighthouse
The Meadow	Headlands
Cathedral Woods	Gull Cove

35

DINE AT DIMILLO'S

A national magazine once said Portland has more restaurants per capita than any place in the United States No one in Maine argues with that assertion, yet, in the burgeoning, beautiful scene of farm-to-table, vegetarian, ethnic, experimental, and upscale restaurants, one stands out. Because it floats.

DiMillo's On the Water should really be called DiMillo's In the Water, because it's a repurposed car ferry moored at Long Wharf. It's 206 feet long, 65 feet wide and weighs 700 tons (before diners are added). There's a huge steam engine, but it's never fired up while diners are present.

With three interior dining rooms and three outside decks capable of seating more than 600 guests at once, DiMillo's is one of the largest boat-based restaurants in the country and the only one in Maine. The vessel bore three names during service as a ferry in three states, and a stint as a boat storage and clubhouse for a yacht club before the DiMillo family bought it.

Open seven days for lunch, dinner, and Sunday brunch, DiMillo's sports, unsurprisingly, a nautical decor, many different lobster options, and an extensive seafood menu. However, the menu also includes non-seafood meals, and, true to the family's origins, many pasta and Italian dishes. Lunch is served from 11-4 and dinner is served all day.

Established in 1954, the business is still owned by the DiMillo family. At least four family members hold management positions. Since the dining areas are neat and clean, founder Tony DiMillo must have been referring to the kitchen, when he famously said, "If you're not making a mess, you're not doing it right."

HELPFUL SITE

- *dimillos.com/restaurant/*

DiMillo's didn't actually start out as DiMillo's. Tony DiMillo opened Anthony's on Fore Street in 1954, where he coined his slogan, "The clams you eat here today slept last night in Casco Bay." Anthony's moved to Center Street in 1960, then to a spot across the street from where the floating restaurant is now. In 1978 the family bought the dilapidated Long Wharf, and the now-famous floating restaurant bearing the family name followed in 1982.

36

GET OFF THE GRID AT A SPORTING CAMP

Hunting, fishing, snowshoeing, snowmobiling, cross-country skiing, ice-fishing, dog-sledding, hiking, birding, or just photographing the wilderness—Maine has sporting camps and wilderness lodges to accommodate all these activities and more.

Since Maine is 90 percent covered in forest and sparsely populated—especially upcountry in the Great North Woods—wilderness is pretty easy to find. Maine's sprawling wilderness also claims many rivers, lakes, and ponds—nearly 13 percent of the state is covered in

fresh water. In fact, some camps are only accessible by water—or seaplane.

Camps and lodges run the gamut from rough and rustic to charmingly, comfortably rustic, and can be found just about anywhere in the state. There's something for everyone from tenting in the wild, to rental cabins with stone fireplaces, to B&Bs with all the comforts of home.

A popular wild area for visitors is the 93-mile long Allagash Waterway region, bordering the 3.5 million=acre North Maine Woods. Rafters, canoists, and recreational fishermen like to explore the rivers; while hunters visit the woods to bag big and small game such as moose, deer, black bear, grouse, and woodcock.

The region surrounding the forever-wild Baxter State Park near Greenville and Moosehead Lake is another popular spot that includes the West Branch of the Penobscot River and the Big Eddy salmon pool.

No longer just for the hook-and-bullet crowd, sporting camps have had to adjust to changing times and tastes. In addition to traditional hunting and fishing activities, most camps are open for just about anything you can think to do in the wilderness. Many are owned or staffed by

Maine Guides to ensure your trip goes just as you planned. And many camps also offer boat rentals.

So, pick your comfort level and your favorite activity. Dress appropriately for the season. Allow plenty of time to get there (wherever it is, most of these places are *remote!*). Perhaps the best source to start with is the Maine Sporting Camp Association

HELPFUL SITE
mainesportingcamps.com

37

WALK IN THE GARDENS

Sure, they're seasonal—Maine isn't the tropics—but if you catch them at their peak, the Coastal Maine Botanical Gardens in Boothbay are spectacular.

Sitting on 270 acres of tidal shore land, the Gardens adds a newly planted area each year, an ever-changing display of art, as well as a permanent sculpture collection by regional artists. The Botanical Gardens also offers art exhibits, talks, tours, and other programs in the visitor center. The Children's Garden, replete with fairy tale buildings, features activities such as puppet shows and encourages the making of fairy

OTHER PUBLIC GARDENS WORTH A VISIT

Asticou Azalea Garden, Northeast Harbor
Thuya Garden, Northeast Harbor
Wild Gardens of Acadia, Bar Harbor
Merryspring, Camden
Vesper Hill Children's Chapel, Rockport
Viles Arboretum, Augusta
Sunken Garden, Wiscasset
The Rose Circle, Portland
The Longfellow Garden, Portland
Longfellow Arboretum, Portland

houses in the nearby woods. There are miles of trails to walk among the gardens and shuttles are also available to help you get around more quickly. There's even a dock where you can take a one-hour boat tour.

Although they are carefully cultivated, all the various gardens look a bit wild, as if they had simply occurred in nature—that's intentional. You can wander between the Woodland Garden, the Perennial and Rose Garden, the Burpee Kitchen Garden, the Clever Event Lawn, the Great Lawn, and the Lerner Garden of the Five Senses. Early winter offers "Gardens Aglow," when the gardens are decked out in holiday lighting and visitors stroll in the evening dark oohing and aahing.

Other than the Gardens Aglow event, the Gardens are open April 15 through October 31, daily 9 to 5.

HELPFUL SITES

- *mainegardens.org*
- *gardenpreserve.org/asticou-azalea-garden/*
- *gardenpreserve.org/thuya-garden*
- *merryspring.org/gardens-grounds/gardens/*
- *mainehistory.org/house_overview.shtml#gardenvilesarboretum.org/*

38

BECOME A CHAMPION TOBOGGANER

That's right. It may not be an Olympic event, but Camden, hosts the United States National Toboggan Championships every February at the Camden Snow Bowl. Since 1991, 2-, 3-, and 4-person teams have braved the 400-foot, frozen toboggan chute, with a vertical incline of more than 70 feet, on which toboggans reach speeds up to 45 miles per hour. It may not be for the faint of heart, but it's a heck of a lot of fun.

While it is technically a championship event, with professional teams competing from all over, it's also open to just about anyone with a team and a toboggan. More than 400 teams compete annually and the event takes on a bit of a festival atmosphere. Most teams have funky names and some dress in silly costumes. There are tents from area vendors serving hot cocoa, coffee, and snacks, and there's usually a chili and chowder cook-off and some music by local talent.

Always held the first weekend in February, weather permitting, you'll want to register your team early. Racers vie for the fastest time down the chute in qualifying and final runs, with a shiny trophy for the winning team. Don't worry if you don't feel like a daredevil. There's always a crowd of people just there to watch and enjoy the scene. It's a good cure for cabin fever.

HELPFUL SITE

- *camdensnowbowl.com/toboggan-championships/*

THE U.S. NATIONAL
TOBOGGAN
CHAMPIONSHIPS

39

MEET MAINE'S FIRST PEOPLE

Some 21,000 years ago, the Laurentide Ice Sheet scraped across Maine, leaving the convoluted shoreline and lots of the rocks we have today. Its aftermath also left habitable land that Paleo-Indians, or nomadic "Red Paint" people, began to inhabit nearly 13,000 years ago. Those first natives were replaced by the Armouchiquois in southern Maine, the Etchemin in mid- to northern Maine, and the Abenaki in the interior

and west. These were the precursors of our modern Maliseet, MicMac, Penobscot, and Passamaquoddy tribes.

PETROGLYPHS

There are several petroglyph (rock carving) sites in Maine, dating from pre-historic times to contact with Europeans. The islands and shoreline around Machias Bay are considered one of the most important concentrations of petroglyphs, with many of the sites listed on the National Register of Historic Places. The carvings were created by picking or carving the surface of the rock to create images.

According to the Maine Historic Preservation Commission, Machias is home to nineteen petroglyph sites. The best known is called the Picture Rocks, considered the most important and sacred site in Maine. These drawings are between 3,000 and 5,000 years old and some may be as old as 10,000 years.

Machias petroglyphs include images of European sailboats coming to shore, one with a cross near the boat, indicating the natives' understanding of Christianity as a separate religion from theirs. Some vessel images are so detailed, individual boats have been identified by scholars. Since images were carved by shamans, or holy men, animal depictions—often deer and moose—indicate possibly asking the spirits for good luck on the hunt, or paying respect to the animals.

To protect their integrity, none of the sites are mapped and they are under the protection of the Maine Coast Heritage Trust (MCHT). Land around the Picture Rocks was returned to the Passamaquoddy tribe in 2006, after 400 years. Guided kayak tours to explore some of the petroglyphs of Machias Bay are available out of Machias, since they can be viewed from the water. MCHT hopes to develop a management plan that balances daytime recreational use of some of the protected properties with the needs of tribal people and archeologists.

Inland, Lovell is the site of drawings depicting humans, including two stick-like figures with raised arms. The technique used to create these drawings is called "pecking" or "dinting" with the artists probably using a stone tool. The site, about 1,000 years old, is a rock formation overlooking a lake in an area frequented by the Abenaki.

ANCIENT MIDDENS

Middens, or shellfish shell heaps, help archeologists ascertain the habits of long-ago shore dwellers. Maine has or had many middens—up to 38 were identified in 1891 and later archeologists counted as many as 2,000 on the coast of Maine ranging from 2,000 to 4,000 years old—but some were destroyed before their historic worth was determined and protections could be put in place. One in York, in southern Maine, also contained human bones, indicating possible cannibalism.

The largest and best-known midden is in Damariscotta, called the Whaleback Shell Midden. This pile of oyster shells was once more than 30 feet deep, and also includes other artifacts from Native American life, including animal and fish bones, ceramic pots, and stone tools. In 1692, some of the midden was used to make lime to build Fort William

WHALEBACK SHELL MIDDEN STATE HISTORIC SITE

MAINE DEPARTMENT OF CONSERVATION
DAMARISCOTTA RIVER ASSOCIATION

WHO WERE THE RED PAINT PEOPLE?

No one knows for sure because so few sites have been found, though it's believed they were among the first people to live here after the Ice Age. Their name comes from the red ochre pigment found in the few grave sites that have been unearthed. They were most likely coastal dwellers who lived off the sea. Since the Ice Age, sea level has risen and the prime archaeological sites for the Red Paint People are probably deep underwater.

Henry in Pemaquid. More was used as fertilizer and road fill, but the largest amount of the midden was removed in the late 1880s when a factory turned the shells into chicken feed. The site is now managed by the Damariscotta River Association as a State Historic Site. There are hiking trails, interpretive panels explaining the area's history, and beautiful views of the river.

Researchers believe this midden may represent at least 1,000 continuous years of use by Native Americans. In 1886, Harvard's Peabody Museum purchased the rights to artifacts found there. Arrows, ax heads, ceramic pots, and the bones of extinct species, such as the great auk, were sent to the museum. Some of the oyster shells found measured more than a foot long.

HELPFUL SITES

- *machiasport.org/points-of-interest/*
- *damariscottariver.org/trail/whale back-shell-midden-state-historic-site/*
- *mainestatemuseum.org/learn/ schedule_a_tour_or_program/ museum_tours_and_gallery_programs/*
- *newenglandhistoricalsociety.com/ the-red-paint-people-of-maine/*

40

RIDE IN A SEAPLANE

For four days every September, the town of Greenville, on the edge of Moosehead Lake, is the site of the International Seaplane Fly-In.

Usually held the weekend after Labor Day, the fly-in is more than four decades old. In the winter of 1973, when their regular clientele of sportsmen was sparse, some bush pilots decided to invite a few more pilots in to spend a weekend flying and having fun.

Enough fun was had to lure more pilots to Greenville in subsequent years, making the fly-in an annual event. In 1995, the International Seaplane Fly-In became a non-profit association aimed at promoting fellowship and fun, including the fly-in itself.

These days, the event attracts more than the usual modern, working seaplanes. Many rare, classic, and experimental planes attend as well. A 1944 Grunman Goose even showed up once and there's the unique site of a DC-3 on floats. Watching the planes may be sufficient entertainment for many. Others will want to climb aboard.

Seaplane rides are available, not just during fly-in, but all the time. Rides range from fifteen-minute tours to tours of Baxter State Park that can take an hour and a half. Moose-watching tours and drop-offs to hiking, golfing, or fishing spots are also available.

The fly-in is accompanied by other events, including plane races, a canoe/seaplane race (don't ask!), and a 5k foot race.

Greenville, a town of around 1,800, attracts several times that number during the fly-in, so it's best to plan ahead for accommodations.

HELPFUL SITE
• *seaplanefly-in.org/general-info.html*

41

DRIVE A STANLEY STEAMER

Sorry, you can't actually drive a Stanley Steamer, the steam-powered car invented by enterprising twins Francis and Freelan Stanley of Kingfield, but you might be able to ride in one.

The brothers produced the first Stanley Steamer in 1897, and over the next two years they sold 200 cars, more than any other American automobile manufacturer. In 1899, they drove a Steamer up Mount Washington, the first car to make the 7.6-mile climb. In 1906, their steam-powered racer set a world speed record for the fastest mile by an automobile—28.2 seconds at 127 mph. This record was not broken until 1911, and wasn't broken by another steam car until 2009.

The Stanley Motor Carriage Company produced the best-known and best-selling steam cars until 1924, when the gasoline-powered internal combustion engine usurped the steam engine.

DRIVING THE STEAMER

The Stanley Steamer was started with a crank, and it had no transmission or brakes. Acceleration was accomplished by stepping on a bar. Letting up pressure caused the car to slow down or stop. It was, however, quite efficient, as only a little kerosene was needed to heat the water to produce steam. And since horse troughs were ubiquitous, a fill-up was never a problem.

Today the Stanley Steamer lives only in museums and the collections of fans, including former *Tonight Show* host, Jay Leno. Visitors to the Stanley Museum in Kingfield will see not only cars, but other interesting inventions. Owners of Stanley cars often participate in a Steam Car Tour that sometimes stops at the museum.

The Owls Head Transportation Museum in Owls Head has a few Stanley Steamers. It might even be possible to catch a ride in a Steamer there at one of the museum's special summer events. The Cole Land Transportation Museum in Bangor also has a Steamer in their collection.

HELPFUL SITES

- *stanleymuseum.org*
- *owlshead.org*
- *colemuseum.org*

42

EAT AT MOODY'S

You don't eat at Moody's Diner in Waldoboro because it's a five-star restaurant full of trendy ambiance. You eat at Moody's Diner because it's a roadside icon with food that hasn't changed basically since forever—predictable diner food.

While the food may not have changed, the building has over the years. From its humble beginnings as a lunch wagon, it has grown and grown to accommodate its always-increasing numbers of fans.

Famous for its whoopie pies, and real pies, Moody's also has a permanent daily special, one for each day of the week.

Not just a traveler's mecca, Moody's has always enjoyed a huge loyal following of local folks—many go for the daily special. Those who love meat loaf appear regularly on Tuesdays, for instance.

Moody's has been steadily expanding on its Route 1 site since it was established. Descendants of the original owners still own and operate the diner. Reportedly two dozen family members still work in the business. There's a Moody's cookbook available to purchase if you wish to reproduce some iconic dishes at home, and an adjacent gift shop carries all sorts of Maine memorabilia.

Any morning of the week you will find the counter and booths filled with locals catching up on news and gossip. Listen carefully and you might hear some classic Maine lingo and stories to go with the classic food. It's a trip.

HELPFUL SITE

- *moodysdiner.com*

WHAT'S ON THE MENU

While there have been additions to the menu over the years to accommodate changing tastes, Moody's traditional dishes are listed under "classics" on the menu. The menu pretty much covers the Maine food gamut, from lobster rolls and clam chowder to ham salad sandwiches and fried tripe. But you can also order a "By Thunder Burger" piled high and stuffed with onion rings.

43

STAND IN THE CLOUDS

The Penobscot Narrows Observatory, located at one end of the Penobscot Narrows Bridge that connects the town of Prospect to Verona Island, is the first bridge observatory in the country, and at 420 feet, the tallest one in the world—taller than the Statue of Liberty.

With its award-winning, innovative design, the observatory offers a 360-degree view of the Penobscot River and surrounding environs. The 100-mile radius of visibility means that on a clear day you can see Cadillac Mountain in Acadia, the Camden Hills, and even Katahdin. The 13-by-25-foot observation room has plaques under

each of the four glass walls to indicate direction and maps of the view.

The observatory is shaped like the Washington Monument and is built into one of the two major support structures for the 2,120-foot state-of-the-art bridge that replaced the old Waldo-Hancock Bridge in 2007. The fastest elevator in Northern New England wings you skyward 400 feet in under a minute, then there's a climb of about three dozen steps to the top.

Along with the sweeping overland vistas, the view of the Penobscot River running through a steep gorge directly below the observatory is pretty impressive. When it opened in 2007 the observatory quickly became the midcoast's most popular attraction. The observatory is open May 1 to October 31 and shares admission with Fort Knox. Turn off Route 1 onto Route 174 on the south side of the bridge for parking and admission. Additional parking is available along Route 1 across from the Route 174 intersection. Knock two off your list in the same day.

HELPFUL SITE
- *fortknox.maineguide.com*

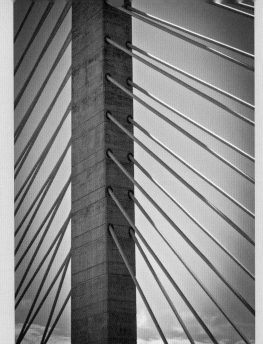

The $89-million bridge is a marvel of engineering and is one of only two bridges in the United States that employs a cradle system, meaning the cable strands are carried from the bridge deck inside long tubes called stays, eliminating the need to anchor the cable in the pylons.

The innovate design allows individual cable strands to be inspected, then removed and replaced if necessary, while other cable bridges require removing entire groups of cables at once. The cable-stay tubes are sealed and filled with super-pressurized nitrogen gas to help prevent corrosion.

44

HIKE THE CANYON

The "Grand Canyon of Maine," properly known as Gulf Hagas, is in the mountains of Central Maine.

Take a day trip if you're within a reasonable driving distance. Or plan to camp out to enjoy the scenic delights—the gorge, waterfalls, swimming holes, cliffs, and old-growth forest. Or, if you're hiking the toughest stretch of the Appalachian Trail—Maine's 100 Mile Wilderness—you'll already be going right past.

Getting to the rim of Gulf Hagas involves a nearly 8-mile hike, starting with a 4.1-mile hike from the parking area on the K-I Road to Stair Falls, and a 3.3=mile return hike along the Pleasant River Tote Road. The Gulf Hagas Rim Trail involves crossing both the Pleasant River (bring waterproof shoes) and the Gulf Hagas Brook. Both crossings can be risky in high water. The first scenic splendor, a half-mile in, is the Hermitage, a stand of beautiful old-growth pines. About a mile after that comes Screw Auger Falls.

Located within the Appalachian Trail corridor in northern Piscataquis County, in a place with the unlikely name of Bowdoin College Grant, East Township (T7 R10 NWP), Gulf Hagas is 15 miles northwest of Brownville Junction. One of fourteen National Natural Scenic Landmarks in Maine, it is owned by the National Park Service.

There are campsites available near the Gulf. While you're in the area, you might want to hike more of the hundred miles of trails through the Ki-Jo Mary Forest, a consortium of privately and publicly owned land managed for recreation by the North Maine Woods, Inc. company.

HELPFUL SITES

northmainewoods.org/ki-jo-mary/gulfhagas.html
mainerec.com/katahdin.asp
mainewoodstourism.org/waterfalls/
gulf-hagas-area/gulf-hagas/

Gulf Hagas is a 3-mile-long slate gorge cut by the West Branch of the Pleasant River as it drops nearly 400 feet.

WHILE YOU'RE IN THE AREA

Check out the Katahdin Iron Works, a state
park and historic site. Iron ore was once
smelted there and the remains of a smelter and
a charcoal kiln can still be seen. In days of yore
logs were driven through the gorge to provide
wood for the smelter, sometimes getting stuck
in the narrower portion of the gorge known
as The Jaws. When the smelter closed, drivers
continued to float logs through on the way to
paper mills.

45

TAKE A DRIVING TOUR OF THE SOLAR SYSTEM

Did you know Maine has a solar system, our solar system, complete with Pluto, which isn't even considered a planet anymore? It's not a real solar system, of course, but it is the largest three-dimensional scale model of the solar system in the world. Even at a 1:93,000,000 scale, the model stretches for 40 miles along Route 1 between Houlton and Presque Isle.

Pluto is a mere 1 inch in diameter and can be found inside the Houlton Information Center at the end of Interstate 95. Its moon (yep, even the moons are included) Charon is a half-inch in diameter and sits about 8 inches from Pluto. Traveling north on Route 1 toward Presque Isle, keep your eyes peeled for the other planets. Jupiter and Saturn are each a couple feet in diameter and are mounted on posts beside the road. Little old Earth is the size of a golf ball and is mounted on a post at Percy's Auto Sales, only a mile from the sun. And the sun, even at this small scale, is 50 feet in diameter. Arc sections are mounted in the halls of the Northern Maine Museum of Science.

HELPFUL SITE

- *pages.umpi.edu/nmms/solar/*

DON'T FORGET EARTHA

On your way north to view the solar system, take a break and stop in at DeLorme in Yarmouth to check out the world's largest rotating globe of Earth. Eartha is in a large three-story atrium and can actually be seen from I-295 North. Its motor is programmed to turn the 41-foot-diameter globe at the same speed (scaled down) that Earth rotates. Eartha is even tilted 23.5 degrees, just like its older brother. There's no charge to view Eartha, but the atrium is only open during DeLorme's business hours.

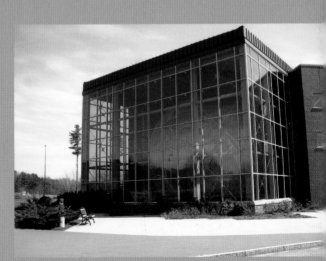

WHERE TO SEE THEM

Cobbosseecontee Lake (also called Cobbossee) in Winthrop

Moosehead Lake in the Greenville area

Various sites in **Acadia National Park**. Rangers often close certain areas to protect breeding loons.

In and around **Baxter State Park**.

Togue Pond

South Branch Pond

Upper South Branch Pond

46
LISTEN TO LOONS

The lonely cry of the loon is distinctive and haunting, and Maine is one of the places where you can hear it in the summer. The unmistakable cry of the loon is more often heard at night, although early mornings and afternoons the birds often indulge in some communication.

Loons are shy. They don't like to be close to people or activity, so keep your distance if you're observing them, especially if they have chicks. And loons need territory. Breeding pairs will defend around 100 acres of space. Loon numbers in Maine, as elsewhere, have dwindled over the past thirty years due to factors besides development: Mercury contamination, lead poisoning from ingested sinkers, boat collisions, and entanglements in fishing line have all harmed loons.

Maine loves loons. Since 1993, the loon has adorned a conservation license plate. And the loon image can be seen in gift stores on T-shirts, pillows, mugs, key chains, and other paraphernalia. Artists and photographers love loons, too.

HELPFUL SITES

- *maineaudubon.org/wildlife-habitat/the-maine-loon-project/ gorp.com/parks-guide/travel-ta-birdwatching-acadia-national-park-baxter-state-park-bar-harbor-sidwcmdev_055474.html*
- *nps.gov/acad/learn/photosmultimedia/upload/Loons.mov*
- *baxterstateparkauthority.com*

A RIDE IN THE PARK

Acadia National Park offers many crushed-rock carriage roads, where bicyclists share the road with horses and walkers. No off-road biking is allowed at Acadia. Some roads are fairly congested and therefore risky, such as the road up Cadillac Mountain.

Mountain biking is a great way to see Baxter State Park, but cyclists are restricted to maintained roads in order to preserve the park's wilderness. The 41-mile-long dirt and gravel Perimeter Road, also known as Park Tote Road, winds through many pristine and beautiful settings. Watch out for moose.

JOIN THE CROWD

Take a long ride and raise money for a worthy cause. The annual **Trek Across Maine,** a three-day tour in June, supports the American Lung Association; and **Bike MS: The Great Maine Getaway,** held over two days in August, supports the National Multiple Sclerosis Foundation. **Bike Maine** is an annual seven-day trek hosted by the Bicycle Coalition of Maine in mid-September. Riders cover an average of 55 miles a day along the rocky coast, through small towns, enjoying great local fare.

47

HOP ON A BIKE

Rated the second most bike-friendly state by the League of American Bicyclists, Maine offers bikers spectacular scenery, friendly and helpful residents, and lots of good food to rejuvenate a tired cyclist. You can explore the woods and byways of Maine by bicycle on the road, off the road, or in nearly any combination imaginable.

Several companies offer bike tour packages around the state for cyclists of different interests and skills, ranging from those who seek challenging terrain (we have a lot of that), to those looking for easier, family-friendly jaunts. Bike clubs throughout the state post their free weekly jaunts. Islands are popular with cyclists and it's easier to get a bike than a car on a ferry without a reservation during the busy summer months.

There's certainly no shortage of places to ride. You could just bring your bike and head out on your own, or you can plan your own bike tour using Maine's Department of Transportation website, ExploreMaine.org.

HELPFUL SITES

- *nps.gov/acad/planyourvisit/bicycling.htm*
- *exploremaine.org/bike/*
- *bikemaine.org*
- *katahdinmaine.com/mountain-biking/149-mountain-biking-in-baxter-state-park*
- *action.lung.org*

48

EXPLORE THE OLD PORT

Portland's Old Port is aptly named, being old and located at the center of Portland's active working harbor. The area lay in disuse until the 1970s, when a revival began. After you've taken a gander from the Portland Observatory (#5), head down Congress Street to explore the trendiest part of this vibrant little city.

You'll walk past the Eastern Cemetery (the city's oldest, dating from 1668), where noted Maine abolitionists and military heroes from several wars are buried. Stop and take a look at the Civil War Monument on the grave of Union volunteer Alonzo P. Stinson, who died at age 19 at the Battle of Bull Run, July 21, 1861. A granite bedroll sits atop the marker for the first Portland casualty of the Civil War.

When you hit India Street, you'll see the first few of the many, many restaurants that crowd this section of the city harbor's edge. India Street has Italian and Japanese restaurants.

Take a right off India onto Middle Street, where nearly every doorway is a restaurant—some with a national reputation and others that deserve to have one.

Head down to Commercial Street (on the water) and just keep walking until you find something that interests you, everything from speciality pizza, Irish fare, endless seafood-chowder-oyster-lobster places, high-end dinner places, fishermen's breakfast joints, DiMillo's floating restaurant (#35), sushi, pubs, and pan-Mediterranean spots.

At a right angle to Commercial Street, there's Dana Street, very short but home to three restaurants. At the end of Dana, turn onto Wharf Street, where you'll find several more, including a bar specializing in chocolate.

While you're wandering in search of food, and trying desperately to figure out how many different kinds of meals you can possibly consume rather than be forced to make a single choice, you may also stop and shop in the many boutiques of the Old Port.

It's a toss-up whether there are more shops or restaurants. Exchange Street, in the center, runs at a right angle to Commercial, all the way up to Congress Street. Here you'll find designer clothing, jewelry stores, specialty boutiques, coffee shops, art galleries and . . . more restaurants.

HELPFUL SITE

• *portlandmaine.com/explore-downtown/*

49

HARVEST ICE

In the early 19th century ice cut from Maine's frozen rivers and ponds was a commodity, traded and shipped by merchants to places as far away as the West Indies. Harvest ice, you ask? Indeed. Once a good thick layer had formed, usually by mid- to late January, crews would go and saw out large blocks. The blocks, weighing upward of 300 pounds, were then guided to shore, hauled out, and stored in the icehouse.

You can relive the history, and break your back in the process, by joining a modern-day ice-cutting operation—though they still use traditional tools. The small village of South Bristol and its Thompson Ice House Harvesting Museum host an annual ice harvest. Attendees can join in the sawing of the ice on Thompson Pond, transporting blocks, stacking them in the icehouse, or simply watching. There's a bit of a festival atmosphere and hot dogs, soup, chili, hot cocoa, coffee, and baked goods can be had. Plus, it's a good cure for cabin fever.

If you're not a winter outdoors person, you can go to the museum in July for their annual ice cream social. The ice cream is made from ice harvested the previous winter. At the museum you can learn all about the history of ice harvesting and the equipment that was used. Times vary depending on the weather, so check the website for dates and museum hours.

HELPFUL SITES

- *thompsonicehouse.com*
- *woodsholemuseum.org/icehouse/inmaine*
- *theheartofnewengland.com/ LifeInNewEngland-Ice-Harvesting*

A MAINE COMMODITY

Who knows for sure when the first ice was harvested, but it became big business in the early 1800s when Boston merchant Frederic Tudor designed icehouses and ice boxes and began shipping ice to the West Indies. By 1891 Charles Morse of Bath had consolidated all the ice trade of the northeast, including the Hudson River, under his American Ice Company, earning him the moniker, "Ice King."

50

SEE THE MILKY WAY

On a clear night in Maine you can look up and see something you can't see from most other places on the Eastern Seaboard—the Milky Way, that large cloudy splash of stars across the sky. Larger, well-lit urban areas have so much light pollution that viewing the full spectacle of the night sky is difficult.

Acadia National Park is one of the best places in Maine to view the Milky Way. The population is fairly small and Acadia and Harbor have passed an ordinance governing the types of lighting allowed. Most light pollution comes from older-style lighting so reducing light pollution requires using directional lighting such as LEDs. Acadia is noted by the International Dark Sky Association as a place that's been successful at reducing light pollution.

There's an annual Acadia Night Sky Festival toward the end of September every year, with workshops, speakers, and, of course, informed stargazing. The Festival describes

Acadia as having "the largest expanse of naturally dark sky east of the Mississippi."

Another place to view the Milky Way without a lot of fuss is also Down East—Curtis Cove in East Blue Hill. This spot is suggested for people who don't necessarily want to camp out, but just wish to park their car on the side of the road, get out, and observe the heavens, weather permitting.

Night sky photographers recommend getting 25 to 50 miles away from major urban areas. In Maine, few population centers are major or urban, so remote places are not too hard to find. The tips of some of the many peninsulas along the coast can make for good viewing.

HELPFUL SITES

- *astro.umaine.edu*
- *usm.maine.edu/planet*
- *acadianightskyfestival.com*
- *asnne.org*

WHEN TO LOOK

The best times to see the Milky Way are when the moon is new, at least two hours after sunset or before sunrise, and especially from midnight to 3 a.m. If you can stand the cold, winter is the ideal time when the air is crystal clear.